Impossible Knowledge

Conspiracy theorists claim impossible knowledge, such as knowledge of the doings of a secret world government. Yet they accept this impossible knowledge as truth. In effect, conspiracy theories detach truth from knowledge.

Knowledge without power is powerless. And the impossible knowledge claimed by conspiracy theorists is rigorously excluded from the regimes of truth and power – that is not even wrong. Yet conspiratorial knowledge is potent enough to be studied by researchers and recognized as a risk by experts and authorities.

Therefore, in order to understand conspiracy theories, we need to think of truth beyond knowledge and power. That is impossible for any scientific discipline because it takes for granted that truth comes from knowledge and that truth is powerful enough to destroy the legitimacy of any authority that would dare to conceal or manipulate it. Since science is unable to make sense of conspiracy theories, it treats conspiracy theorists as individuals who fail to make sense, and it explains their persistent nonsense by some cognitive, behavioral, or social dysfunction.

Fortunately, critical theory has developed tools able to conceive of truth beyond knowledge and power, and hence to make sense of conspiracy theories. This book organizes them into a toolbox which will enable students and researchers to analyze conspiracy theories as practices of the self geared at self-empowerment, a sort of political self-help.

Todor Hristov is a critical theorist based at the University of Sofia, Bulgaria.

Conspiracy Theories
Series Editors: Peter Knight
University of Manchester
Michael Butter
University of Tübingen

Conspiracy theories have a long history and exist in all modern societies. However, their visibility and significance are increasing today. Conspiracy theories can no longer be simply dismissed as the product of a pathological mind-set located on the political margins.

This series provides a nuanced and scholarly approach to this most contentious of subjects. It draws on a range of disciplinary perspectives including political science, sociology, history, media and cultural studies, area studies and behavioural sciences. Issues covered include the psychology of conspiracy theories, changes in conspiratorial thinking over time, the role of the Internet, regional and political variations and the social and political impact of conspiracy theories.

The series will include edited collections, single-authored monographs and short-form books.

Impossible Knowledge
Conspiracy Theories, Power, and Truth
Todor Hristov

Impossible Knowledge

Conspiracy Theories, Power, and Truth

Todor Hristov

Routledge
Taylor & Francis Group

LONDON AND NEW YORK

First published 2019
by Routledge
2 Park Square, Milton Park, Abingdon, Oxon OX14 4RN

and by Routledge
52 Vanderbilt Avenue, New York, NY 10017

First issued in paperback 2020

Routledge is an imprint of the Taylor & Francis Group, an informa business

British Library Cataloguing-in-Publication Data
A catalogue record for this book is available from the British Library

Library of Congress Cataloging-in-Publication Data
A catalog record for this book has been requested

ISBN 13: 978-0-367-67029-0 (pbk)
ISBN 13: 978-1-138-34682-6 (hbk)

Typeset in Times New Roman by Apex
CoVantage, LLC

Contents

Introduction

Conspiracy theories were fairly unfamiliar to my country before 1989.

They were popularized by Nikola Nikolov, a Bulgarian emigrant in the United States. I met him once in the quasi-baroque hallways of the University of Sofia. I was a student back then. He said that he had just arrived from the land of the free and asked me about the cafeteria. While we were enjoying our tripe soups, a Balkan delicacy with a dubious reputation, he told me all about the secret world government and offered a seductive discount on his book *The Global Conspiracy* (Nikolov 1990).

"How do you know all this?" I remember asking him. Nikolov explained that he was a reader in the Library of Congress. Later that day, after some research, I found out that the Library of Congress was publicly accessible, and I wondered how it was possible to discover the secrets of the world government in a public library, particularly if many paid with their lives for trying to disclose them, as Nikolov had mentioned.

Now I know that conspiracy theorists often claim to know the impossible, such as the doings of a secret world government. The goal of this book is to explain why. It is intended as an introduction to conspiracy theories from the perspective of critical theory, or, from a different vantage point, as an introduction to critical theory from the perspective of conspiracy theories.

Critical theory is an interdisciplinary field of knowledge organized around the discursive practice of critique. For the purposes of this book, we can define critique as an art of voluntary insubordination that involves questioning the truth of power and the power effects of truth through tactical articulation of singular, situated, subjugated knowledge of struggles (Foucault 1997, 32, 2004, 8). Or perhaps we can define critique by its effect:

> [T]he immense and proliferating criticizability of things, institutions, practices and discourses; a sort of general feeling that the ground was crumbling beneath our feet, especially in places where it seemed most familiar, most solid, and closest to us, to our bodies, to our everyday gestures.
>
> (Foucault 2004, 6)

Critical theory provides scattered comments rather than systematic analysis of conspiracy theories. However, reading critical theory from the marginal perspective of conspiracy theories offers at least two advantages:

1 Such an approach can put conspiracy theories in a different perspective. They are usually analyzed as beliefs, narratives, or representations, but conspiracy theories are also acts, and the concepts outlined in this book enable one to analyze their pragmatics and dramatics, i.e. how their meaning is modified by the situation and how they modify their situation and their subject (Foucault 2008, 68).

2 The approach can lead to an alternative problematization of the nexus of knowledge, power, and truth. We often take for granted that knowledge is founded on authority and associated with truth, but conspiracy theorists claim to know the impossible. So, their impossible claims are dislodged from power and truth. Although these claims are not a hard currency, conspiracy theorists still ascribe to them the value of knowledge.[1] How is it possible to value as knowledge impossible claims beyond power and truth? If you think that this question is relevant only to conspiracy theorists, then you should take into account that impossible knowledge claims are quite more common than conspiracy theories. Take for example a venture capitalist who claims knowledge of the returns on investment in a future technology that may never come into existence; or a middle-aged office worker who desperately seeks to know where his life went wrong, as if ordinary lives break only at a single point; or a housewife consumed with anxiety about the personal and financial costs of changing her life by abandoning herself to the pleasures of eating, praying, loving, and the most expensively priced of all – tourism; or a student who needs to know if she made the right choice by investing years of her life as well as a significant amount of student loan debt in an education that could be easily made redundant by the labor market. Unfortunately, in our professional, personal, social, or everyday lives, we can easily find ourselves in a double bind, in which it is impossible to know and at the same time impossible not to know, or at least impossible to bear not knowing. Yet this double bind is unthinkable by means of the conventional concept of knowledge embedded in authority and truth. Then, if we take into account such impossible situations, what is knowledge?

Since this book is intended as an introduction, and since it approaches critical theory from the marginal perspective of conspiracy theories, the theories are read from an unusual angle and simplified. But simplification is not merely a diluted version of the same. Theories are dense and delicate textures made of concepts, arguments, examples, rhetorical figures, narrative patterns, indexical expressions, and seemingly auxiliary phrases like *in fact, in effect*, and *essentially*. To simplify a theory means to disentangle some of its components. In effect, their meaning becomes loose. It can be fixed only by the reader, but in order to do that, she has to use them in her own language games; hence, the meaning of the disentangled components depends on their potential use. In that sense, simplifying a theory implies transforming it into an abstract diagram or into a model.[2] Notwithstanding its obvious shortcomings, such simplification has at least three important advantages:

1   It represents theories as toolboxes that cannot be thought of independently of their use.
2   The disentanglement of components opens up gaps that were perhaps filled by rhetorical devices, modes of emplotment, or auxiliary phrases, and in that sense it opens up new lines of problematization in what could otherwise seem a seamless texture.
3   Theory today is often perceived as "the freemasonry of useless erudition" (Foucault 2004, 5). Simplification undermines that perception because it does not let one rely on the convenient assumption that one's knowledge is not problematic and cannot be problematized. If simplification is tactically felicitous, it can make critical theory more self-critical, and it can transform it from erudition into experience, perhaps even affect.

To simplify a theory means to rework it, and although this work is supposed to be as indiscernible as the work of a good reproduction painter, if it is productive, it deviates irredeemably from the original. Yet I hope that even though the simplifications attempted in this book are not accurate reproductions, they are not untrue to their originals, as they are motivated by fidelity. However, I have tried to give extensive references to the original texts, and I recommend reading this book against their background.

The book consists of three chapters and a conclusion. The first chapter tries to explain the conspiratorial claims of impossible knowledge by social suffering; the second chapter, by desire. The third chapter examines conspiracy theories as acts of speech formed by and transforming relations of power. The first chapter includes discussions of the concepts of sublime and cognitive mapping developed by Frederick Jameson; justification, test, and reality, developed by Luc Boltanski; irrationality and ego weakness, developed by Theodor Adorno; order and risk, formed under the influence of Michel Foucault. The second chapter outlines Adorno's concept of bi-phasic syndrome, the concept of ressentiment introduced by Friedrich

Nietzsche and later developed by Max Scheler and Marc Angenot, the Lacanian concepts of fantasy and passage into act, the concept of symbolic efficiency introduced by Slavoj Žižek, and the concepts of empty signifier and hegemony proposed by Ernesto Laclau. The third chapter uses the concepts of parrhesia, subjugated knowledge, race war, spirituality, techniques of the self, and truth, formulated by Michel Foucault, and tries to rearticulate them in parallel with the concepts of knowledge and truth defined by Alain Badiou, the concept of passionate utterance invented by Stanley Cavell, the concept of seduction proposed by Jean Baudrillard, and the concept of diagram developed by Gilles Deleuze and Félix Guattari.

Each chapter is divided into smaller sections, and the theoretical sections are usually followed by a discussion of a particular case of conspiracy theory. The cases are supposed to demonstrate how the concepts can be used as analytical instruments and to problematize them from the perspective of practical situations, i.e. to show how the concepts both overcome and pose singular problems that cannot be reduced to theory. Indeed, the theoretical argument of the book is shaped by such singular problems brought by the instrumentalization of concepts, rather than by theoretical concerns.

The conspiracy theories discussed in the book are not the weird beliefs we are so used to ridiculing. They are about risks, distrust, capitalism, corruption, suffering inescapable as fate, and disasters prepared in secret. I hope that they will demonstrate the intricately overdetermined situation and the ambiguous, often undecidable effects of conspiracy theories. But, of course, you can also find in the book stories about aliens who have replaced the president with a cyborg or prescribed universal sexual liberation.

In conclusion to this introduction, I would like to thank to my colleagues in the COST action CA1510 "Comparative Analysis of Conspiracy Theories," whose inspiring and challenging voices reverberate in this book.

Notes

1 On conspiracy theories as a regime of knowledge production, see Butter 2014, 27; Birchall 2006, 21, 34; Dean 1998, 176.
2 I am referring to the concept of diagram in Deleuze 1988, 72–3, and to the concept of model in Tenev 2017.

Bibliography

Birchall, Clare. 2006. *Knowledge Goes Pop*. Oxford: Berg
Butter, Michael. 2014. *Plots, Designs, and Schemes: American Conspiracy Theories from the Puritans to the Present*. Berlin: Walter de Gruyter
Dean, Jodi. 1998. *Aliens in America: Conspiracy Cultures from Outerspace to Cyberspace*. Ithaca: Cornell UP

Deleuze, Gilles. 1988. *Foucault*. Minneapolis: Minnesota UP

Foucault, Michel. 2008. *The Government of Self and Others: Lectures at the Collège de France 1982–1983*. New York: Palgrave Macmillan

Foucault, Michel. 2004. *"Society Must Be Defended": Lectures at the Collège de France, 1975–1976*. New York: Picador

Foucault, Michel. 1997. *The Politics of Truth*. Los Angeles: Semitoext(e)

Nikolov, Nikola. 1990. *The World Conspiracy*. Sofia [Николов, Н. 1990. *Световната конспирация*. София: Изд. авт.]

Tenev, Darin. 2017. "The Models of Poetics", *Textpraxis* 3

1 Suffering

This chapter argues that conspiracy theorists make impossible knowledge claims because they suffer.

But if conspiracy theorists were suffering from a broken mind or body, they would simply be ill. Their impossible knowledge claims should have deeper roots in the in-between space, in which individual bodies and minds converge or diverge, conflict or synchronize. In a word, their suffering should have social roots.

Of course, some diseases affect populations rather than isolated individuals, and conspiracy theories were once indeed considered a sort of epidemic that spread through the contact of dangerous minds like the far-right extremists or the communists. But the conspiratorial narratives gained such wide currency in late modern popular culture that their conceptualization as an epidemic or even as a pathology no longer seems adequate.

The ground of order

Conspiracy theories have been explained by the suffering caused by the flawed social order of late capitalism.

Since the concept of order is often used as an empty abstraction, let me illustrate its concrete stakes by means of an example discussed by Michel Foucault in the introduction to *The Order of Things* (2002, xix–xx).

After World War I, Kurt Goldstein and Adhémar Gelb invented a test for abstract thinking (Gelb and Goldstein, 1920; Finger et al. 2009, 248–9): the subject was asked to sort a large number of woolen skeins of varying color and texture. If the subject was suffering from color anomia, she would endlessly arrange and rearrange the skeins; for example, she would group them according to hue, but then she would scatter them again in order to group them according to brightness, only to start shifting them about from one place to another in a fraught attempt to take into account their texture, until she would heap them up again in the center of the table.

Neurologists explain color anomia by a lesion of the brain. But Foucault used the color sorting test as an illustration that any order rests on a ground, without which words and things fall apart. So, from a Foucauldian perspective, what is wounded in the case of color anomia is not just the brain but the ground of order. If the anomic subjects cannot stop ordering and reordering the skeins, it is because any order they manage to produce seems to be ungrounded, a thin foil of orderliness covering an unfathomable disorder.

Foucault's example also demonstrates that the ground of order is not a given; it is a product of labor. To order a heap of woolen skeins means to put them in their places, but to do that one needs to divide the multiplicity into elements, to decompose the common space of the table into different places, to differentiate the time of ordering into moments like 'first,' 'second,' 'next,' 'after that,' etc., to assign a proper place and moment to each element, to decide which elements belong or do not belong together, to decide which elements are similar or dissimilar, and – since they are linked not by binary relationships of equivalence or opposition, but rather by an intricate web of resemblances and differences – to define the threshold between relevant and irrelevant resemblances and differences, to decide on the threshold beyond which the differences between two elements become too much to put them together or the resemblances between them are enough not to pull them apart, to organize the differences between the elements of a group into an open series of variations of the same, to take into account the distance and proximity between the different groups of elements, to set up residual and hybrid groups like 'the rest,' 'unsorted,' 'to be taken care of later,' without which any order is impossible or at least impractical, and so on.[1]

In a nutshell, the ground of any order is the work of ordering. Although in the case of the color sorting test, ordering is a relatively uncomplicated work for one, it can be much a more extensive, sustained, sophisticated, collective effort which involves a multiplicity of agents and intricately organized and stratified apparatuses of power, production, signification, and subjectivity (Foucault 1988, 17; Agamben 2009, 2–15).

Anomia

Many critical theorists have interpreted conspiratorialism as a symptom of a flaw in the late capitalist social order identified with its incomprehensible totality, complexity, social contradictions, powerlessness, and injustice.[2]

But if we take into account that conspiracy theories make social totality even more incomprehensible, that the critics who explain them as symptoms of the social situation do not take into account their heterogeneous functions in popular culture and often sound conspiratorial themselves, then such diagnoses would justifiably seem nothing but theories of conspiracy theories which are too powerful for their object, which reduce power to repression, and which are themselves inscribed in the grand plot of class struggle (Knight 2000, 20, 74, 225, 2003, 23).

I argue that it is more productive to read such theories as arguments that late capitalism affected the very ground of social order, the work of ordering. Even if we admit that the social order is a given, it will not be incomprehensible if we cannot grasp it. And to grasp it means to order it for ourselves, from our perspective. Of course, that does not mean to draw an accurate or detailed map of the social order, just like we do not need a map to understand indexical expressions like 'here,' 'now,' or 'we.'

For an ordinary actor, to comprehend the social order means to find one's place in it. But in order to do this, one needs to sort out a multiplicity of elements that are quite more complicated than a heap of woolen skeins, at least because of the following reasons:

1   They are cumulative quantities that cannot be decomposed into individual units, just like a traffic jam cannot be decomposed into individual cars.

2   They are variable, quite like the number of cars needed to jam the traffic at a particular point.

3   The elements of the social order are differential, i.e. they are defined by differences or thresholds, as the traffic jam is characterized by its difference from stopping at a red light, or by the threshold below which the cars just move slowly.

4   The elements of social order depend on a series of other variables which are open, unpredictable, interdependent, and often unknown (a traffic jam depends not only on the place and the time of the day, but also on the road network and its condition, on the public transportation network, on the share of car ownership by household, on the weather conditions, on the current events – perhaps a football game, a renovation, a police blockade, etc.; Foucault 2009, 35–7; Garfinkel 2002, 92).

Comprehending the social order is a sophisticated practical accomplishment, even if it depends on fuzzy categories like 'us' and 'them,' on questionable figures like 'the aliens,' or on heterotopia like 'the Balkans.' Late capitalism has made this accomplishment increasingly difficult, for at least the following reasons:

1   The ground of modern order was shaped by disciplinary apparatuses (Foucault 1979; Jameson 1988, 349). If we simplify, to order a multiplicity of elements means to put them in a closed space, to impose on it a grid that allocates an individual place to any element, to organize the

elements according to their function or value, to measure their deviation from a norm, and to organize them into spatial or temporal series, so as to maximize efficiency (Foucault 2009, 67–9). If you find that description abstract, then any modern classroom or cubicle office can provide an ample illustration. Now, in late capitalism the grid of disciplinary order has been eroded by flows that are deterritorialized in the sense that they cannot be closed up in a delimited space, like capital, information, or migrant flows, and in consequence ordering has come to mean putting in their places elements that circulate beyond borders at an increasing velocity (Jameson 1988, 350–1).

2   Late capitalism is driven by the imperative of growth. But to achieve exponential growth, one needs to intensify production at increasing rates. Since the products have to be put in circulation, the demand for them should be virtually insatiable. So, the crucial products of late capitalism are not the tangible goods of the modern industry, like machines or clothing, but rather goods that make a difference, like novelties or brands. In order to survive, late-capitalist industries need to produce differences with increasing intensity (Jameson 1991, 4). In effect, to comprehend the social order one has to sort out series of cumulative differential elements that develop at an increasingly higher speed. Imagine a Gelb-Goldstein color sorting test in which the psychologist keeps putting new wool skeins on the table faster and faster, the color of the skeins depends on their difference in hue from others, so they increasingly change their colors, and perhaps the table is shaking.

Of course, social order is still comprehensible, if not to the ordinary actor, then at least to a critic like Frederic Jameson or to his critics. But such critics have at their disposal the powerful discursive apparatuses of social science and critical theory. The poor[3] do not have access to such sophisticated and expensive apparatuses of knowledge production, and if they do not develop faster than late capitalism, they are unable to put their social world in order and they become socially anomic.[4] However, that does not mean that they give up and live in disorder, but rather that just like the color anomics, they are consumed with an incessant, desperate, increasingly productive work of ordering which is never arrested in a finished product, an endless reordering disentangled from any order, an act without knowledge (Foucault 1988, xii).[5]

To be socially anomic means to be unable to find your place among the others. But this does not mean to be excluded, to lack a place and in that sense to be free. It means that your position is constantly sliding, that your place is always becoming something else, that you are always elsewhere.

And although that can be invigorating, since you can always hope to end up in a different place (Jameson 2009, 595), it can be also frustrating because you will always be displaced and misplaced (Dean 1998, 11).

Demanding the impossible

How do impossible claims of knowledge articulate social anomia?

Almost two months after the start of the occupation of Zuccotti Park in 2011, Occupy Wall Street made no demands. The mainstream media reproached the protesters that if they demanded nothing, the authorities could not offer them a thing, so they could achieve nothing and they would be responsible for their unavoidable failure.

A special working group discussed relentlessly the list of demands of the movement. A few days before Thanksgiving, at a decisive but not very well attended meeting, the group reviewed the final version of the list, which was now reduced to creating jobs. In the course of the discussion reemerged other demands, like nationalization, reduction of student debt, and establishment of a party. Then a new member of the group known as Elk said:

> Of course, we'd love to get rid of debts, and have jobs. But people in this country with money and power are deciding policy outside of government, in a way to support people with money.
>
> (Demands 2011a)

Was this a conspiracy theory? Or just a general dissent? Was it different in kind from the demand to nationalize the banking system proposed by a communist a few minutes before? Itzak, an older member of the working group, asked Elk what people he had in mind and how he came to know about their secret dealings. So Elk explained:

> This is through my own research. . . . My understanding is that [they are] members with a lot of money, and they tend to be members of the Bilderberg Group, Trilateral Commission, and the Council on Foreign Relations, members of these groups are often members of other groups, and they are the people coming together and committing treason, because they are creating policy and not allowing the two party system to work.
>
> (Demands 2011a)

Now, this was obviously a claim about a small group of powerful people conspiring together to advance their interests by means of secret manipulation of public institutions (Knight 2003, 15). Conspiracy theory, commented Itzak later on, and in response Elk made an even more impossible claim:

> The problem with conspiracy theories is that they are not just theories. These things are true. They are conspiracy facts. That is something that the general public doesn't know much more about. There needs to be education. I think this movement is about everyone taking personal responsibility for choices that we have made. Therefore we all need to educate ourselves. So we understand that these aren't conspiracy theories. When you look at Building 7 and see what architects and engineers say, there's no question that the government had something to do with 9/11.
>
> (Demands 2011a)

Elk's claim was impossible not simply because of its contents. Its subject was constituted by impossibly idiosyncratic knowledge. It was addressed to the potential 'we' that would emerge out of the transformation of his idiosyncratic knowledge into social norm. The actual listeners, the members of the working group, were reduced to ears that should hear his address to this actually nonexistent 'we.' And Elk was demanding the impossible, in a language that made the others doubt his seriousness or sincerity, in violation of the accepted procedure, as he did not wait for the proper item in the agenda and spoke too long. But is not this the formal structure of any revolutionary discourse?

Nevertheless, the claim was made by a subject unable to speak properly, to a subject that could not hear, through the channel of tens of ears that did not want to hear. And because of this triple impossibility, the truth of the claim or the right to make such a claim was not even questionable. The claim was not even wrong (Bratich 2008, 3), and the only question was how could one wrong the truth so much, how could one violate the right to speak this much?

And since the claim seemed a wrongdoing, the question was not what Elk wanted to say, but what made him talk like that. Suffering, perhaps.

The conspiratorial sublime

Conspiracy theories can be explained as an attempt to repair the anomic situation brought about by late capitalism.

In general, such theories postulate an order hidden beneath the social order. But the hidden order should belong to the social order, because otherwise it would be irrelevant. At the same time, it should not be included in

the social order, because otherwise it would be carried away by the incessant displacement of social positions.

Conspiracy theorists solve or dissolve the paradox of belonging without
inclusion by representing the hidden order as a totality (Jameson 2009, 603,
1992, 3, 1991, 38). Indeed, the totality of a multiplicity of elements belongs
to the multiplicity without being included in it, just like the totality of a city
belongs to the city without being a part of it (Jameson 1988, 353).[6]

But if totality is hidden, if it is lacking from the present social order, it cannot be represented, hence it cannot be communicated, even if one believes
strongly in it. In fact, if one believes strongly in it, this would amount to
a delusion. Therefore, in order to curb the anomia of late capitalism, conspiracy theorists need to represent the unrepresentable. And because of that,
the mechanism of their theories can be captured by the concept of sublime
(Jameson 2009, 594–5, 1991, 5)

Sublime is precisely the representation of what cannot be represented.
Take for example a storm, the power of which holds one in awe. If one would
try to represent its power, she would fail because she had been overpowered
by the storm, and even the greatest power would not be an overpower. So,
she can represent the absolute power of the storm only negatively, as a failure of her power to represent it, indeed as a failure of her faculty to imagine
it. Yet, precisely because of that, she will be able to experience in herself
a powerful faculty which exceeds even the power of imagination – reason,
which ideas can only posit an absolute power or an all-encompassing totality. As a result, the storm will trigger a deep and ambiguous affect which
will combine both pleasure and pain – the pain of the failure of her faculty
of imagination and the pleasure of the experience of her faculty of reason
(Lyotard 1991, 98–9, 1994; Žižek 1999, 40–1; Kant 1961, 109ff).

Conspiracy theories have developed two modes of representation of the
unrepresentable totality of the social order (Jameson 2009, 603). The first
mode represents it as a system which controls or consumes everything
and everyone, a machine of power that makes one lose any hope (Jameson 2009, 603, 1992, 5). The second mode represents the hidden totality
of social order as an event that makes one experience history itself – a
crisis or a revolution in which anything seems possible. Each mode of
representation brings about a characteristic type of affect – melancholia
and horror in the first case, pathos and enthusiasm in the second (Jameson
2009, 596).

However, the conspiratorial sublime has fundamental flaws.

1   Both modes of conspiratorial representation as well as the associated
    types of affects are not disconnected. Conspiratorial theorists usu-
    ally swing between their poles (Jameson 2009, 593), so in effect they

escape the incessant sliding of the social order at the price of an incessantly sliding affect.

2   The impossible totality represented by the conspiracy narratives involves a characteristic concept of time. Normally, the meaning of a moment in time depends on what has passed and what comes next. But the time of sublime machines or events is detached from the flow of moments. They are not determined by the future; they determine the future and perhaps even the historical past. In that sense, the meaning of their time is immanent, which is also one of the defining features of utopia (Jameson 1992, 45, 2009, 612). Therefore, conspiracy theories have a utopian dimension. But since they represent a sublime power that is inherently oppressive, conspiracy theories are dystopic (Jameson 2009, 420). And if we take that into account, we can oppose them effectively not by debunking their impossibility but by developing utopias which open up alternate worlds of emancipation (Jameson 2009, 609–12).

3   Conspiratorial representations of sublime power provide imperfect cognitive maps of the social order which mislead about the suffering they are supposed to relieve (Jameson 1988, 356,1991, 38,2009, 9). In order to explain that, let us take again the example of the city. It is a multiplicity of elements, but we still imagine it as one. The one, however, is not given to experience because we can never experience the city as a totality. So, the city-as-one implies a work of ordering which transcends experience and which we can call cognitive mapping (Jameson 1988, 353, 1992, 2, 2009, 594–5). Now, conspiracy theorists read any actual cognitive map as a surface which hides another map of a virtual field of forces (Jameson 2009, 595). So, they read even the city landscape as a virtual battlefield, and because of that, they overlook the actual battles for the right to the city, fought on a daily basis by each of us. More importantly, conspiracy theorists try to relieve the incessant sliding of social positions by displacing the actual social order on the virtual plane of a hidden order, the rationale for which is war.

#Occupy sublime

Are affective oscillation, dystopic temporality, and virtualization of social landscapes merely flaws of conspiratorial narratives, or are they cracks in the narratives, gaps opened up by the narratives, which uncover a deeper layer? I do not know much about Elk.

Elk is just a nickname. I could not trace it even to an #Occupy forum user, and it does not appear elsewhere in the proceedings of the Demands working group of Occupy Wall Street, or the New York City General Assembly.

If we follow the contextual clues, we can assume that Elk was young, that he did not come from money, he did not have a college education or a steady job, and he could be called a gentleman with a touch of irony:

> John: What this young gentleman, god bless him, he's here, at least people come out to be heard. Doesn't matter if you agree or disagree. When I make a statement I try to base it off some facts.
>
> (Demands 2011a)

Elk can be probably categorized as a member of that particular stratum of the working class which Marx called the reserve army of labor, possibly of its deepest layer called the paupers, whose labor is depreciated to such an extent by the development of technology that even if they manage to sell it, the value they will get will not cover their costs of living (Marx 2003, 703–10).

However, to categorize by social position means to describe a place in the social order, and thus to prescribe a part in a community, to ascribe a part of the common good, and to inscribe a life trajectory (Ranciere 1999, 5–6). If Elk was indeed a pauper, the price of his life would be paid by others, perhaps by his relatives or by the welfare system; the most valuable part of the common good he would get would be retail credit; and the trajectory of his life would gradually but steadily decline together with his vitality. Should we be surprised then that Elk was trying to escape his social position?

Elk argued that social order was merely superfluous because the real class conflict was hidden underneath its surface. Marxists define classes by their relationship to the means of production. If we simplify, capitalists own the means of production, landowners and financiers own sources of rent, and proletarians need to sell their labor in order to live. Late capitalism has washed out that grid of concepts because the most important means of production and sources of rent became intangible, they are owned mostly by multinational corporations, and even the most successful senior executive officers sell their labor. So, Elk claimed that the real means of production was the money and the real class conflict was between those who owned the money and those who needed money. And since the class of money-owners is sociologically inconceivable, since it cannot be even named properly, Elk represented it by means of an allegory (Jameson 1992, 67), as a list of names like the Bilderberg Group or the Trilateral Commission associated by a web of small resemblances, for example being non-governmental organizations that bring together people with power and money for informal discussions closed to the general public, in houses with the reputation of influence.

Hunter, a Marxist member of the Demands working group, was understandably frustrated. He argued that the core problem was who controlled the means of production, that it should be controlled by the people, but since the people were not awakened, the #Occupy movement should establish a political party. Anything else would play into the hands of the capitalists, said Hunter (Demands 2011a). Yet his counterargument depended on the categorization of the social position of those who owned the money as capitalists. Elk believed that the counterargument missed the point because, to Elk, those who owned the money did not occupy a definite social position, as they were the machine of power which controlled everything.

The sublime power of this total or totalitarian machine was difficult to represent because it could easily indicate depression rather than oppression. In trying to avoid that risk, in his short interventions Elk oscillated between his anger and the enthusiasm brought about by the #Occupy movement, an event that seemed to interrupt the course of time and made one feel that history was happening now, that what was happening now was of global significance, a sublime event. Elk claimed passionately that we should educate ourselves, we should take responsibility, we should change the world, I had expected more of you. And it would soon turn out that his enthusiasm was counterbalanced by a utopia – to discard all the money and distribute the global resources according to the needs by means of a sublimely intelligent computer, whose artificial nature would free it from self-interest and immunize it against injustice.

From the perspective of Frederic Jameson, it should be somewhat surprising that the utopia of artificially intelligent non-capitalist economy did not undermine the dystopic theory of an elite that secretly controls everything through money but rather operated as an associated milieu which provided a source of additional energy (Deleuze and Guattari 1987, 51). However, overwhelmed by the enthusiasm of the sublime event of a potential revolution, the Marxist Hunter abandoned his opposition.

Still, why was the map of the hidden class conflict between those who owned and those who needed the money unreliable? Was it because, although it was good enough to lead Elk to Zuccotti Park, it would not help him return to a different place after the end of the occupation and would not change his social position? Or was it because Elk tried to map out the unreliability of social order?

Anxiety

The impossible knowledge claims of conspiracy theorists can be also explained by anxiety (Boltanski 2014, 15, Dean 1998, 7, Adorno 1994, 127, Fenster 1999, 40–1).

Anxiety is perhaps a feature of any social order. However, in modernity it was shaped by the national state, in particular by its instruments for settling disagreements (Boltanski 2014, 20). In order to explain that, let me turn once again to the color sorting test (Boltanski and Thévenot 2006, 32–3).

Imagine that instead of passively following the directives of the psychologist, the subject starts to argue that the color, which the psychologist deems to be green, is actually brown. The classification of a woolen skein in one category rather than another depends on associations, and the psychologist and the subject of the experiment have associated the same skein with different colors.

In natural situations, every element holds together, and the associations of all the elements of the situation are shared by all (Boltanski and Thévenot 2006, 35). But this is obviously not a natural situation. How could the psychologist and the subject resolve their disagreement?

Firstly, they can both relativize the situation by ignoring the presence of the other and by focusing on the circumstances (Boltanski and Thévenot 2006, 32). Secondly, they can settle on a common association like greenish brown or brownish green (Boltanski and Thévenot 2006, 33). But the first approach would break up the common situation, and each would be alone even though they are before the eyes of the other. The second approach would imply that the psychologist had cast aside her authority and started to negotiate with the subject on an equal footing.

If those approaches do not seem feasible, the psychiatrist and the subject can try to transpose their argument to a more abstract level (Boltanski and Thévenot 2006, 33). Of course, that could lead to an infinite regression to ever more abstract categories. But the parties in the argument can avoid the infinite regression by settling for a more general principle, for example, that the color of the skein should be defined on the basis of its difference from the color of other skeins, or that the color should be defined on the basis of its dominant hue. And both general principles will be essentially regimes of equivalence between the skeins, the color of which differs in the same way from the others, or between the dominant hues of a group of skeins (Boltanski and Thévenot 2006, 40).

If the psychiatrist and the subject refer to different general principles, they can resolve their conflict by means of a test. And in this context, to test does not mean to make an object reveal its truth. It rather means to use objects to reveal whose principle is truer, to establish the truth-value of each principle against the other, and hence to estimate the ability of each party to evaluate the object of the test against the ability of the other party. Normally, the principle that wins the test is considered justified, and this resolves the disagreement. If, for example, the subject manages to justify the general principle according to which the color is brown, then this is just the color of the woolen skein. But to transform a disagreement into agreement about what is just the case means to do justice, and in that sense the psychologist and the subject accomplish justice (Boltanski and Thévenot 2006, 34, 40).

Now, the modern state has aspired to be the ultimate test of reality, and the conspiratorial anxiety is generated by the defects of its test. To make that more understandable, let us make the following distinction between reality and the real: the real is a lived experience, and therefore it is open, incoherent, ambivalent, in a constant state of becoming; the reality on the other hand is tested, and therefore it is articulated as a set of justified general forms, norms, and procedures (Boltanski 2014, 15).

The modern state needed to test reality because, unlike the premodern states that crystallized around the problems of war, peace, and justice, it was driven by the imperatives of maintaining order, accumulating wealth, and intensifying life (Foucault 1997, 94). And to test reality, the modern state needed instruments which would enable it to arbitrate between competing claims, to measure values, and to identify risks. Driven by that need, the modern state developed such powerful instruments as bureaucracy, the sciences, and statistics (Boltanski 2014, 17).

However, the general principles justified by such instruments never came to be powerful enough to become the only versions of reality (Boltanski 2014, 21). And the order articulated by the instruments of the modern state was being constantly destabilized by the tensions between the territorial nature of the state and the deterritorialized flows of capital, between the volatility of economic positions and the stability of social positions, between equal civil rights and social inequality, between the public interest pursued by the state and the conflicting private interests (Boltanski 2014, 22–4).

What was more, the reality, which was guaranteed by the modern state, was framed as a totality that transcended any individual experience, just as the administrative protocols invented by bureaucracy or the public opinion produced by statistics transcended any individual state of mind. In order to be represented, this totality had to be communicated, and so it depended on words. But the words of the representatives of the state were inherently ambivalent because, although their subject of enunciation was the state, they were uttered by individuals, which entangled the questions of who was speaking, in whose interest, or whether those who spoke in the interest of the state were actually speaking in their private interest (Boltanski 2014, 20).

The tensions invited the public to question the reality of reality, to look for tests intended to establish the truth about the gaps between individual and institutional experience, about the risks lurking in those gaps, about the vulnerability of the social order produced by the modern state or the need to protect it by self-imposed states of exception, and ultimately to prove the truth about the real that escapes the state reality (Boltanski 2014, 18–20, 202).

In effect, the tests of reality developed by the modern state became increasingly inconclusive, and distrust and suspicion were progressively extended to cover the whole social order (Boltanski 2014, 21). That produced social anxiety about the reality of reality, which was tapped first by detective novels, then by spy novels, and more recently by conspiracy theories (Boltanski 2014, 39, 198). Later all those genres of suspicion, particularly the conspiratorial narratives, infused popular culture, gained wider currency than the state version of reality, lost their overtones of crying and raging from the margins (Fenster 1999, 50), and shifted their function from articulating identity to articulating risks that hide in the interstices of the reality produced by the state (Knight 2000, 32, 229, 2003, 23).

The real of the occupation

How is it possible to test an impossible knowledge claim? And what if the tests of reality fail?

In October 2011, the facilitators of the Demands working group gave a couple of interviews in which they mentioned the creation of jobs through an extensive public works program as the principal demand of Occupy Wall Street.

The facilitators of the General Assembly accused them of trying to take over the movement, deleted the page of the working group from the NYC General Assembly website, and denounced it in a post on the #Occupy forum (Occupy 2011; Richard 2011).

The working group tried to justify the demand by using the instruments for production of reality, on which the late modern state had long ago lost the monopoly. At first the facilitators resorted to statistics, but the data were inconclusive (Demands 2011b). So, at the meeting on November 17, one of the working group members, Susan, reported that she had consulted the demand with three economists, who were "broadly supportive." Then Elk interrupted the organizational talk of the facilitators:

> It seems like a moot point for me. . . . It seems like jobs will correct themselves when other things are taking place. Like getting money out of politics. When we see that trilateral commission (and other actors) agree with the way the economy is run. My question is that, I feel it's important for us to address questions that are the root of the problem. Getting money out of politics.
>
> (Demands 2011a)

The discussion was sidetracked by other interruptions intended to propose other demands, until Elk interrupted it again with a claim about what was real:

> Hi, while I love what is being discussed here, I am kind of shocked because I feel they are very naive, because they will all be taken care of when we get the government back from corporate interest. The core issue is getting money out of politics.
>
> (Demands 2011a)

Now the attempts of the facilitators to settle their disagreement about what was to be done were transposed to a more abstract level, the level of general principles. But how was it possible to justify the principle that money should be out of politics?

One of the working group facilitators, Jay, objected that such a general principle could not be tested because testing it would require a series of impossible objects like capitalist enterprises which maintained their production without any prospect of profit, or clandestine elite groups submitted to public regulation (Demands 2011a).

Since the principle of getting money out of politics could not be tested, the facilitators could not resolve the disagreement by a reference to the version of reality already justified in the context of #Occupy, by expert opinions, or by statistical instruments. Their disagreement with Elk was whether a problem that escaped their attention was real.[7]

And as the disagreement made them question the reality of their reality, it brought about anxiety, which added to the initial anxiety of an unexpectedly unattended meeting. Since anxiety is objectless, unlike fear, it can easily overflow, and it seems that this soon affected even the young Elk, who took the floor once more to express the general worry that the next meeting would be even less attended because it was close to Thanksgiving.

However, anxiety about reality cannot be contained without resolving the question about the real that escapes it, and such a question cannot be resolved without a plot (Boltanski 2014, 24). Another facilitator, Erik, wrapped it in yet another question implicitly addressed to Elk: what was the source or the organization that came up with his demand?

The question implied a secret group that tried to hide its clandestine agenda behind the face of Elk. Was that another conspiracy theory? If we go beyond the celestial realms of literature and social theory, is the disagreement produced by one conspiracy theory resolvable only by another conspiracy theory?

One last problem: was not the potentially conspiratorial question, articulated in the mode of debunking, actually a form of violence, to the extent that Erik did not recognize the need to justify himself (Boltanski and Thévenot 2006, 38)?

Risk

In our everyday lives, we need to make calculations. But they are more like correlation functions rather than like arithmetic operations on constants. Our calculations involve open series of variables which are inscribed in a complex grid of covariation, depend on confounding or latent variables, and can rarely be represented as stable categories or reduced to measurable quantities.

Take for example someone who wants to be competitive at work. If she is not exceptionally talented, she has to work more than the others. But then she would be stealing time from her family, and if she takes away too much time, the family would probably fade away. However, in her efforts to be more productive, she would be also stealing from her free time, and she would need to compensate for it by more intense forms of pleasure. Let us assume that she starts eating more sweets because that makes her feel that she is doing what she is not supposed to, and in that sense, it gives her the additional enjoyment of emancipation. Still, she could not afford too much enjoyment, because it would erode her health and her labor power, and in the end it would cost her too much. Yet, on the other hand, if she does not get enough enjoyment, she will soon become frustrated, which will erode her vital force and labor power just as unavoidably as the excessive enjoyment, and it will also cost her too much.

Everyday calculations are usually founded on intensive variables like 'more,' 'too much,' 'not enough,' and 'probably,' which often depend not on only the current state of affairs but also on potential events characterized by the probability of some gain or loss rather than by the presence or absence of some fact. In other words, everyday calculations often depend on risks.[8]

Although everyday life has always been exposed to dangers, risk is a modern phenomenon (Foucault 2009, 89; Ewald 1991, 201–5; Hacking 1990, 105–12). Let us take again the example of sugar. It is not a direct cause of illness; it is only a factor correlated with a series of health problems ranging from diabetes to accelerated aging, which are not actual but potential events. In order to evaluate the health risks of sugar, one needs to calculate their probability. A number of brilliant mathematicians after Pascal and Fermat developed methods for calculating probabilities, but in order to work, their methods have to be applied to long series of occurrences like thousands of coin tosses, or in our case, to hundreds of thousands of instances of disease, which were registered systematically only after the advent of the administration of public health in the 18th century (Foucault 1997,

139–41). However, the administration was interested in the instances of disease not so much because of a sense of pity toward the afflicted but because it considered the population a valuable resource, and the insurance market already provided regimes of calculation of the value of lives or working hours lost to disease (Ewald 1991, 205). Also, public hygiene and sanitary science already offered techniques of intervention that would curtail the loss of human capital (Foucault 1997, 150–1).

In sum, knowledge about risks involves a sophisticated apparatus composed of techniques of calculation, methods of administration, regimes of capitalization, and practices of biopolitical intervention that are inherently modern.

The apparatus of risk management seems able to put in order not only an actual situation but also open possibilities, and even if it cannot make the risks disappear, it can make them governable (Foucault 2009, 69). In effect, it has been incorporated in many modern and late modern mechanisms of security, production, or government. The products of risk management have come to be so widely distributed that now even our daily meal is wrapped in risks.

Irrationality

The modern and late modern apparatuses of risk management are also pedagogical devices. They have taught us that our choices are associated with risks.

Of course, in our everyday calculations, risks are not usually turned into numbers because we rarely make use of probability calculus or public health registers. We use the knowledge produced by the apparatuses of risk management as many other apparatuses, on which we rely in our everyday lives – without knowing exactly how they work.

Nevertheless, we know that if we do not know the risks, we are irrational, and if we do not want to know about them, if we want to be irrational, that does not free us from risk; it means only more risk. Then what does it mean to be rational? To behave as if we know what we do not, or to behave as if we do not want to know what we already know?

The problem is further complicated by the fact that if we want to know our place in the social order, we need to know the social order, but late capitalist social order is in a state of constant reordering. If you think that knowing your place is not that important, you should consider at least three further ramifications of the problem:

1   In a capitalist society, to be rational means to pursue one's self-interest. But our lives depend on others whose interests conflict with ours. Then is it rational to relativize the situation by ignoring their presence, as if

each of us lives in our own reality, in which we can pursue our interest unconstrained by others (Boltanski and Thévenot 2006, 32–3)? That is probably the solution advocated by liberalism, but it can ruin what is common; for example, public goods, which range from good trans-portation and good education to a shared concept of good life. Yet, if we compromise our personal interests in favor of the public good, how can we defend our rationality without assaulting capitalism (Adorno 1994, 46)?

2   Capitalism has invented a powerful device for justification: the free market. Take for example the disagreement between producers that sell their products at different prices or between workers that put different value on their labor. As far as the market is free, their disagreement will be resolved by the test of competition that will establish the just price of the product or the true value of labor (Boltanski and Thévenot 2006, 194–6). But even after the 1929 crisis, it seemed that in order to keep the markets free, governments should constantly intervene to free them from monopolies and oligopolies. Since the battle against monopolies and oligopolies turned out to be an endless and endlessly losing war, the markets entered a state of constant reordering, which undermined their functions as tests held sacred by liberalism (Adorno 1994, 154).

3   Modern societies have defined success as social mobility, and social mobility means moving from one social position to another. But if the totality of the social order is incomprehensible and social positions are constantly on the move, how could you know that you are moving for-ward, rather than that the social order is moving against you (Adorno 1994, 85–6)? And if you cannot know if you are moving forward, how can you know that you have accomplished anything or that your accomplishments will not be turned back by the movement of the social order?

It seems that late modern rationality has run amok (Adorno 1994, 46), or that it became autoimmune (Derrida 2005, 34–5). A person with a strong ego could be expected to overcome that autoimmune disorder of rationality by clinging to the concept that she molded her fate, at the price of implicitly accepting the general principle that to be rational means not questioning the irrational social conditions (Adorno 1994, 58).

But what if one's ego is weak?

Ego weakness

A person with a weak ego will still calculate risks, but she will be constantly upset by the irrationality of her calculations. Since she will not feel that she is in control of their outcomes, the outcomes will appear as accidents of fate (Adorno 1994, 57).

Feeling abandoned to fate in a society that calculates even force majeure will probably cause a complex form of suffering, which involves at least the following layers:

1 In our everyday lives, our calculations lead to choices. Since we calculate our choices ourselves, we are responsible for them. So, if her calculations make her choose wrongly, she will be responsible for the negative outcomes. Her calculations will not just be wrong, it is she who will be wrong. In effect, she will experience an unquenchable anxiety at making a mistake (Adorno 1994, 127), which will merge with the anxiety about the real that escapes reality brought about by modern state.

2 Since she will feel her calculations irrational, she will be in a constant search for security. But the search will not lead anywhere; it will seem both irrational and irresistible, and in that sense it will be a mild form of obsessive-compulsive behavior, like coming back a couple of times just after you left in order to make sure you turned off the stove (Adorno 1994, 88).

3 If her fate is not uncommonly happy, she will feel the negative outcomes of her decisions as denials of gratification imposed from the outside by the external power of an oppressive social order. In effect, she will experience frustration (Adorno 1967, 765).[9]

4 But as far as the others do not find the social order oppressive, she will feel isolated (Adorno 1967, 765). Of course, one can be isolated in many ways, but she will not even be isolated as a stranger; she will be isolated as a stranger at home (Horkheimer and Adorno 2002, 105–6). That is perhaps the most wounding kind of isolation because it amounts to an expulsion from the social order that erases her social self and reduces her to bare life, in which she feels dispossessed of everything but her soul (Adorno 1967, 765).

As many other forms of irrationality that have permeated popular culture, for example secondary superstitions like mass-media astrology, conspiracy theories can be explained as defense mechanisms against such ambivalent suffering (Adorno 1994, 47; Habermas 1992, 120):

1 Conspiracy theories can enable one to contain anxiety by transforming it into fear. If that does not seem much of an improvement, take into account that anxiety is hard to fight because it does not have an object, but fear is focused on an object, which one can try to confront, work through, or at least avoid (Adorno 1994, 69).

2   Obsessive-compulsive behavior is driven by questions of 'what if' which got out of control. Usually, the subject is trying to silence them by doing something, but since the questions are irrational, the thing she is doing is closer to ritual than to rational action, which in turn complicates the situation with at least one more question: 'What if I am irrational?' Conspiracy theorists are relieved from that complication because they tend to develop the ritual of snooping, which cannot be told apart from any rationality that does not reflect critically on its motivation (Adorno 2000, 2, 1994, 161; Fromm 2013, 102).

3   Conspiracy theories can counterbalance frustration by a narcissistic desire to know. Since narcissism is essentially an investment of desire in oneself rather than in others, desire to know is associated with unconscious narcissism if it is articulated as desire to be in the know, to know more than others or at least more than others that are unlike you (Adorno 1994, 200; Fenster 1999, 105). Many social theorists like Theodor Adorno and Max Scheler tried to capture that desire to know by the concept of semi-erudition (Adorno 1994, 61; Scheler 2007, 16–17). But we should take into account that semi-erudition is an effect of the redefinition of knowledge as information typical of late modernity, rather than an effect of not reading enough or not reading well enough (Adorno 1994, 161).

4   Conspiracy theories are often blended with prejudice, and prejudice can neutralize isolation. Of course, this is not because it provides reliable knowledge of the stereotyped others, but rather because it articulates a collective subject, a general 'we' associated with 'the nation,' 'the people,' or 'everyone.' That imagined collective subject can support one's inner perspective of the social order as oppressive power, notwithstanding her real isolation; in fact, the more effectively it does so, the more she feels isolated (Adorno et al. 1967, 765).

However, conspiracy theories are flawed defense mechanisms because the suffering they are trying to relieve is caused by the autoimmunization of rationality in late modern societies, and they operate at an individual level.

It is perhaps understandable that, being unable to change the outside world, conspiracy theorists try to change it from the inside (Adorno 1994, 78). But they alleviate suffering by the double move of interiorizing it as a personal fear and exteriorizing it as a hidden order that defies representation. In consequence, they increase the irrationality they are supposed to chase away.

Zeitgeist

Is it possible to fully explain an impossible claim as a defense mechanism? In the context of #Occupy, the demand to get money out of politics was often associated with a surreptitious collective subject, the Zeitgeist movement (Coatesy 2011). The movement emerged out of a 2007 performance by Peter Joseph in which he staged the truth about Christianity, the September 11 attacks, and the banking system. The performance was surprisingly successful, so he made a documentary. The film was available online, and soon it got more than two million views. He tried to channel its popularity by making two more documentaries.

In 2009, Peter Joseph established the Zeitgeist movement. Initially, it was intended as an activist group in support of the Venus project developed by the architect James Fresco. Since I would not like to simplify its conceptual framework, I will use the account of a member of the movement, Nick, who gave an interview at Occupy Chicago:

> The monetary paradigm is basically the foundational structure of our civilization as we know it right now. . . . This monetary paradigm as we know it, as unfortunate as it is, is collapsing as we speak. Now the reason why I say this is because this is obviously apparent anywhere you look if you take the time to look around the world today. . . . As far as the monetary structure goes, the capitalist system that we have now, when we talk about representing the 99%, we talk about representing the vast majority of people who this system does not sustain; (the people) this system does not want to sustain. This system is basically set up to sustain 1% or less of the population, which in this system is the extremely wealthy class and people who just have money, like the owners of banks and stuff like that.
>
> (Faye 2011, 11–13)

In the fall of 2011, #Occupy seemed a potential revolution. As many others, Peter Joseph tried to lead it. In October 2011 he published a video address to Occupy Wall Street, and a week later he gave a lecture at Occupy City Hall and visited a couple of other occupations. The members of the movement created dozens of threads at the #Occupy forum, published innumerable posts, and perhaps communicated even more actively during the occupation.

Joseph's address did not generate the expected response. However, the members of the movement tried to defend his ideas at the working groups, and in the course of the debates they endorsed the demand to get money out of politics. We do not know much about Elk, but we can assume that he supported the demand for reasons similar to Nick's:

> The Zeitgeist Movement is a social awareness movement to educate the public towards the idea of moving towards a research [i.e. resource] based economy. . . . We need a system that sustains all people on this planet. The resource based economic model, after years of researching it myself is how I arrived at this conclusion. . . . It's based on the idea that we have certain human needs to fulfil. If these needs are not met then it leads to deprivation, mental health issues, heart issues, and issues in general. It also leads to problems with inferiority, the class system, structural racism, which are all foundations of the society as well.
> (Faye 2011, 13–14)

One can certainly read this justification of the demand to get money out of politics as an account of a real problem that undermines the reality of the state. The hidden order in the interest of the people who own the money probably operates as a cognitive map of sublime power represented both in the melancholic mode of the system that controls everything and the enthusiastic mode of the event that would change the world – the global revolution triggered by the #Occupy movement. And perhaps Peter Joseph has fueled Nick's narcissistic desire to know more than the educated in spite of his self-education, or his sense of belonging to a global and abstract collective subject.

Yet how are we to explain Nick's passion for a utopia that promises him an unreachable future, or his allegiance to a cognitive mapping that gives him only invulnerable enemies, or his belief in universal education that depends on nothing but desire? In other words, how are we to explain the intensity of his enthusiasm? By the intensity of his suffering?

Are the accounts of suffering enough to explain Nick's anxiety about what will happen to the world, which grows exponentially to his hope for the resource-based economy, or his claim of knowledge about an event that would inevitably happen? Is that event Occupy Chicago, which barely outlasted his interview, or it is yet to come, the global awakening or World War III he mentioned in passing?

And if the event is yet to come, how can he claim to know what is coming? After all, he should justify his claims not only before the others, but also before himself, and he does not even imagine himself as a prophet. If his claim was grounded only in suffering, would he not hear in it a groan rather than the silent steps of the future? What other grounds can a claim of impossible knowledge have?

Notes

1 The work of ordering can be subsumed under the concepts of discernment and classification developed by Alain Badiou (2005, 328–9). Framing the work of ordering in such concepts has the obvious advantage of systematicity. But it can misrepresent the situated, open, and unpredictable nature of the work of ordering, which is a radical phenomenon in the ethnomethodological sense (Garfinkel 2002, 222).

2 See for example Jameson 2009, 596, 1991, 38, 1988, 356; Rosanvallon 2018, 162–4; Boltanski 2014, 22–4; Melley 2012, 5, 2000, 109; Fenster 1999, 40–1; Birchall 2006, 22; Knight 2000, 18; Dean 1998, 6; Adorno 1994, 57.

3 This refers to Jameson's famous phrase that conspiracy theories are cognitive mapping for the poor (1988, 356).

4 Frederic Jameson tried to capture the condition of social anomia by his concept of schizophrenia (Jameson 1991, 26). However, the breakdown of the signifying chain into series of disconnected elements is more characteristic of aphasia, which psychiatrists deem similar yet distinct from anomia. I have tried to simplify this conceptual framework by discussing anomia.

5 Such endless work of ordering can explain the distinguishing features of the late capitalist subjects described by Frederic Jameson – focus on the immediate, orientation toward intensities, private temporality, discontinuity, lack of depth, lack of center, weakened sense of historicity (Jameson 1991, 15–16, 1988, 351).

6 This is a simplified and contextualized version of the concepts of belonging and inclusion in Badiou 2005, 81–3.

7 On the unverifiability of conspiracy theories by juridical or scientific tests, or by consensus, see Dean 1998, 15–16, 170–2.

8 For a detailed analysis of the practical logic of everyday calculations, see Koev 2015; Deyanov 2010.

9 On the relationship between conspiracy theories and powerlessness, see Birchall 2006, 22–3. For a comparable argument that does not take into account the ambiguity of conspiracy theories, see Dean 1998, 173–4. For an argument that conspiracy theories are regimes of imaginary rationalization of powerlessness that perform the cognitive function of representing the causes of suffering, the political function of redistributing the responsibility for it, and the psychological function of compensating for the incomprehensible complexity of modern societies, see Rosanvallon 2018, 162–4.

Bibliography

Adorno, Theodor. 2000. *The Psychological Technique of Martin Luther Thomas' Radio Addresses*. Stanford: Stanford UP
Adorno, Theodor. 1994. *The Stars Down to Earth*. London: Routledge
Adorno, Theodor, Else Frenkel-Brunswik, Daniel Levinson and R. Nevitt Sanford. 1967. *The Authoritarian Personality*. New York: Wiley
Agamben, Giorgio. 2009. *What Is an Apparatus?* Stanford: Stanford UP
Badiou, Alain. 2005. *Being and Event*. New York: Continuum
Birchall, Clare. 2006. *Knowledge Goes Pop*. Oxford: Berg.

Boltanski, Luc. 2014. *Mysteries & Conspiracies: Detective Stories, Spy Novels, and the Making of Modern Societies*. Cambridge, MA: Polity

Boltanski, Luc and Laurent Thévenot. 2006. *On Justification: Economies of Worth*. Princeton: Princeton UP

Bratich, Jack. 2008. *Conspiracy Panics: Political Rationality and Popular Culture*. Albany: New York UP

Coatesy, Tendance. 2011. "The Zeitgeist Movement and Occupy UK." *Left Socialist Blog*, Accessed 12.04.2018, https://tendancecoatesy.wordpress.com/2011/10/31/the-zeitgeist-movement-and-occupy-uk-an-anti-globalisation-cult/

Dean, Jodi. 1998. *Aliens in America: Conspiracy Cultures from Outerspace to Cyberspace*. Ithaca: Cornell UP

Deleuze, Gilles and Félix Guattari. 1987. *A Thousand Plateaus: Capitalism and Schizophrenia*. Minneapolis: Minnesota UP

Demands. 2011a. "Minutes, 11/15 Meeting." Accessed 02.07.2018, https://web.archive.org/web/20111228193038/www.nycga.net/groups/demands/docs/minutes-1115-meeting

Demands. 2011b. "Minutes, 10/27 Meeting." Accessed 02.07.2018, https://web.archive.org/web/20111113141908/www.nycga.net/groups/demands/docs/minutes-from-meeting-october-27

Derrida, Jacques. 2005. *Rogues: Two Essays on Reason*. Stanford: Stanford UP

Deyanov, Deyan. 2010. "The Practical Logic of the Gift: To Think with Bourdieu Against Bourdieu", *Sociological Problems* 42: 268–79

Ewald, Françoiz. 1991. "Insurance and Risk", in *The Foucault Effect: Studies in Governmentality*, edited by Graham Burchell, Collin Gordon and Peter Miller, 197–210, Chicago: Chicago UP

Faye, Hannah. 2011. *Occupy the World: From the Heart of the Protesters*. N.d.: Lulu.com

Fenster, Marc. 1999. *Conspiracy Theories*. Minneapolis: Minnesota UP

Finger, Stanley, François Boller and Kenneth Tyler, eds. 2009. *History of Neurology*. Amsterdam: Elsevier

Foucault, Michel. 2009. *Security, Territory, Population: Lectures at the Collège de France, 1977–1978*. New York: Picador

Foucault, Michel. 2002. *The Order of Things: An Archaeology of the Human Sciences*. New York & London: Routledge

Foucault, Michel. 1997. *Essential Works of Michel Foucault 1954–1984*. Vol. 3. *Power*. New York: New Press

Foucault, Michel. 1988. *Madness and Civilization: A History of Insanity in the Age of Reason*. New York: Vintage

Foucault, Michel. 1979. *Discipline and Punish: The Birth of the Prison*. London: Penguin

Fromm, Erich. 2013. *Man for Himself*. N.d.: Open Road

Garfinkel, Harold. 2002. *Ethomethodology's Program*. Oxford: Rowman & Littlefield

Gelb, Adhémar and Kurt Goldstein. 1920. *Psychologische Analysen Himpathologischer Fälle*. Leipzig: Barth

Habermas, Jürgen. 1992. *Autonomy and Solidarity*. London: Verso

Hacking, Ian. 1990. *The Taming of Chance*. Cambridge: Cambridge UP

Horkheimer, Max and Theodor Adorno. 2002. *Dialectic of Enlightenment*. Stanford: Stanford UP

Jameson, Frederic. 2009. *Valences of the Dialectic*. London: Verso

Jameson, Frederic. 1988. "Cognitive Mapping", in *Marxism and the Interpretation of Culture*, edited by Cary Nelson and Lawrence Grossberg, 347–57, Urbana: Illinois UP

Jameson, Frederic. 1992. *The Geopolitical Aesthetic: Cinema and Space in the World System*. Bloomington: Indiana UP

Jameson, Frederic. 1991. *Postmodernism, or the Cultural Logic of Late Capitalism*. Durham: Duke UP

Kant, Immanuel. 1961. *The Critique of Judgment*. Oxford: Clarendon

Knight, Peter, ed. 2003. *Conspiracy Theories in American History: An Encyclopedia*. Vol. 1. *A-L*. Santa Barbara: ABC Clio

Knight, Peter. 2000. *Conspiracy Culture: From Kennedy to the X Files*. London & New York: Routledge

Koev, Kolyo. 2015. "The World as a Local Affair: Toward the Logic of Situated Practices", *Fenomenologia* 13

Lyotard, Jean-François. 1991. *The Inhuman: Reflections on Time*. Stanford: Stanford UP

Marx, Karl. 2003. *Capital: A Critique of Political Economy*. Vol. 1. *The Process of Capitalist Production*. New York: Cosimo

Melley, Timothy. 2012. *The Covert Sphere: Secrecy, Fiction, and the National Security State*. Ithaca: Cornell UP

Melley, Timothy. 2000. *Empire of Conspiracy: The Culture of Paranoia in Postwar America*. Ithaca: Cornell UP

Occupy. 2011. "Demands Working Group." *Occupy Wall Street*, 21.20.2011, Accessed 16.07.2018, http://occupywallst.org/article/so-called-demands-working-group/

Ranciere, Jacques. 1999. *Disagreement: Politics and Philosophy*. Minneapolis: Minnesota UP

Richard, S. 2011. "Internal Tensions Within Occupy Wall Street: The Demands Working Group and the Drummers' Working Group." *The Charnel-House*, 26.10.2011. Accessed 16.07.2018, https://thecharnelhouse.org/2011/10/26/internal-tensions-within-occupy-wall-street-the-demands-working-group-and-the-drummers-working-group/

Rosanvallon, Pierre. 2018. *Good Government: Democracy Beyond Elections*. Cambridge, MA: Harvard UP

Scheler, Max. 2007. *Ressentiment*. Milwaukee: Marquette UP

Žižek, Slavoj. 1999. *The Ticklish Subject: The Absent Center of Political Ontology*. London: Verso

2   Desire

The impossible knowledge claims made by conspiracy theorists cannot be explained only by suffering because they have a deeper layer which cannot be reduced either to harmful social conditions or to defense mechanisms.[1] The chapter argues that this deeper layer can be problematized as desire. But, in order to do that, we need to conceive of desire not as a fire burning inside but as a discursive economy (Foucault, 1978, 68–9; Deleuze 2006, 124–6).

Reasonably insane

To desire means to work.

Conspiratorial desire, for example, involves reading, looking, questioning, reasoning, interpreting, investigating, explaining, writing, and communicating, all brought together in a personal effort to reorder the world. Perhaps that work is often tacit, as the everyday practices we consider common sense (Garfinkel 1967, 173).

In the first half of the 19th century, the work which we now usually associate with conspiracy theories became a problem for the emerging science of psychiatry.[2] On one hand, it seemed indistinguishable from normal reasoning. On the other hand, it seemed unreasonable because it contradicted the social order and the subject's part in it.[3]

Psychiatrists defined such work as intellectual monomania and hoped to explain it by a lesion in the brain (Esquirol 1845, 320) or by an incompletely cured melancholia or mania (Griesinger 1867, 262). However, the causes of intellectual monomania were difficult to prove, and it rarely deteriorated into complete insanity. So, in the second half of the 19th century, the concept was decomposed into series of lines of problematization. One of them focused on an important distinguishing feature of such disturbed work of reason – the lack of product. It seemed that the reasoning of intellectual monomaniacs did not give positive knowledge and therefore led to nothing, even to less than nothing, because it brought forth claims to knowledge unassimilable to the social order; for example, that one's relatives were spies or that one was persecuted by the Freemasons (Griesinger 1867, 328). In the late 19th century, psychiatrists tried to capture such counterproductive reasoning by the concept of delusion of persecution (Lasègue and Falret 2008).[4]

At the turn of the 20th century, delusion of persecution was integrated into the concept of paranoia (Kraepelin 2012, 425–6). In consequence, it was linked with another line of problematization that emerged from the dissolution of the older concept of intellectual monomania, which associated delusional reasoning with the melancholic idea that everything was lost or that the world was out of joint (Griesinger 1867, 262). The concept of paranoia now enabled psychiatrists to interpret that idea as a delusional attempt to shift the responsibility for one's suffering onto the world (Kraepelin 2012, 425–6, 432–3).

However, the approach of classical psychiatry to the counterproductive work of reason was limited because psychiatric concepts were intended to capture pathologies (Knight 2000, 20–1). But conspiracy theories could also entice normal subjects, and in that case, the intensity of counterproductive reasoning could not be explained by the severity of the mental disorder.

Social mourning

What drives counterproductive reasoning?

Rickey lives a life with no future, in one of the poorest black neighborhoods of Chicago. In this interview, he hints at a popular conspiracy theory, that the authorities conspired to drown black neighborhoods in drugs:

> An' I feel like from 1980 before the drug scene really, really hit – don't git me wrong! Drugs was out there, but there was [very insistent] nothin' near like it was now. An' I feel man, it was like a master plan, ya know. We as people – ya know, black people – we couldn't do nothin' but excel and continue to move forward, ya know what I'm sayin', but when this drug hit us, man! It was like "BOOM!": tha' set us back 50 years, ya know. It's simple as that: it's brother agains' brother. I don't care abou' ya's long as I git mine.
>
> (Wacquant 1999, 165)

What is the function of this conspiracy theory?

If it is a cognitive map, then it shows no way out. If it is intended to represent the real that lurks behind the reality created by the state, then the real is once again the state. If it is a defense mechanism, then it makes the frustration deeper.

It seems that the function of Rickey's conspiracy theory is to articulate what has never been but nevertheless feels lost – his own prosperity lost together with his boxing career and the prosperity of his community and that of all black people in the United States.

Yet how is it possible to feel as a loss what has never been?

This is a work of social mourning, writes Loïc Wacquant (1999, 156). But is it not also a counterproductive work of reason? Where does the work of social mourning take its energy from? Is mourning reducible to suffering?

Ressentiment

The problem of the counterproductive work of reason can be approached if it is reconceptualized as work of desire.

Then the intensity of a delirium of interpretation or a delusion of persecution can be explained by the concept that even though they do not produce any positive knowledge or effect, the subject still derives from them gratification of her desire.

In the early stages of the research on conspiracy theories, the desire that puts conspiratorial minds to work was explained by relative deprivation:

> In every society that is composed of antagonistic groups there is a nascent and descent of groups. . . . The intensification of anxiety into persecutory anxiety is successful when a group (class, religion, race) is threatened by loss of status, without understanding the process which leads to its degradation. . . . Generally, this leads to political alienation, i.e., the conscious rejection of the rules of the game of a political system.
> (Neumann 1957, 290, 293)

Yet conspiracy theories do not compensate for relative deprivation; they just represent it as a result of injustice. So, conspiracy theorists desire not so much the betterment of their situation but rather the condemnation of injustice.

But how can condemnation be an object of desire?

One of the influential phenomenologists of the first half of the 20th century, Max Scheler, tried to solve that question by the concept of ressentiment.

The concept was introduced by Friedrich Nietzsche to describe a reaction that was foreclosed from becoming an act and in consequence turned into a feeling, into a desire of imaginary revenge (Nietzsche 1998, 19–24, Deleuze 2005, 104–9). Scheler tried to rework ressentiment into a sociological concept which can be outlined as follows (Scheler 2007, 2–15; Boltanski 2014, 178–80; Angenot 2013, 8):

- If the status of a social group is considerably lower than its power, as for example in democracy, where formal equality is undermined by social inequalities, then the group feels entitled to more but powerless to change its condition.

- Frustrated by its impotence, the group tries to relieve it by negating the value of the superior groups.
- If the devaluation of others is not acted out as an open conflict, then the group members can develop a value delusion, i.e. a deviant system of values intended to compensate for their inferiority.
- However, the group members cannot detach themselves from the social order without receding into psychosis, so they articulate the delusional values as a hidden order transpiring behind the social order, or vice versa.
- In effect, the group feels the social order irrational and incomprehensible and develops aversion from power and a desire for vengeance that can be fulfilled only in the imagination.
- Since the unfulfillable desire for vengeance makes the group feel even more powerless, this desire is repressed, and if the repression is not strong enough to erase it, it turns into a constantly recurring reaction that forecloses any act and that could not be appeased even by an improvement of the situation.
- Moreover, the improvement would be felt as a further repression because it would contradict the desire for vengeance and deny the compensations provided by ressentiment – the intellectual pleasure to know how the group was wronged and the moral pleasure to know who was responsible.
- However, since ressentiment cannot be appeased by any improvement, it lacks positive content, which distinguishes it from anger, envy, or vindictiveness.[5]

In sum, desire turns into ressentiment if it crosses the threshold of pure repression, beyond which it represses even itself.[6] But if desire involves work, which is supposed to bring gratification, as we have assumed, then the subject of ressentiment derives her gratification from repression.

How is it possible to enjoy repression?

Value ambivalence

Ressentiment is the sentiment of another. Quite like fetishism, it implies a subject of knowledge able to discern the value delusions of others. In practical circumstances, however, it is often difficult to tell perception from misconception.

Rickey's conspiracy theory is intended to explain the powerless condition of his community, which makes civil or political rights seem nothing but a facade hiding the real war of everyone against everyone (Wacquant 1999, 152).

But Mattie, a former friend of Rickey's from a neighboring project, is a success. After a fortunate boxing career, Mattie has managed to move out of the neighborhood to a middle-class area and works as a sheriff and athletic instructor (Wacquant 1999, 155–6).

If the conspiracy theory that the authorities intentionally supported the drug economy is motivated by ressentiment, then it should be grounded on value delusion, and in order to affirm his delusional values, Rickey should be expected to devalue the accomplishments of those who have moved up the social ladder, like Mattie (Scheler 2007, 9–10; Boltanski 2014, 179).

Indeed, the friends who managed to move out of the neighborhood seem to be an object of Rickey's disparagement (Wacquant 1999, 162). But if Rickey is trying to devalue Mattie's accomplishments as well, then why is he indulging in the fantasy that Mattie is running a secret drug ring and living in a high-class building beside the city park (Wacquant 1999, 156)?

Of course, the phantasm can be interpreted as a cognitive map which shows that the only way out of the ghetto is the way of the ghetto, the hustling economy (Wacquant 1999, 143), or that a black man can legitimize his life only if he manipulates the authorities' expectations about reality and hides his illegal activities in a posh apartment.

Still, is not this a phantasm of positive value? Does it not affirm rather than negate the value of Mattie's accomplishments? Does the phantasm not even hyperbolize their value so as to make them translatable in the positive categories of the ghetto?

Or is the phantasm ambivalent, and any attempt to differentiate between its positive and negative contents is misleading? In that case, we need to rework the concept of ressentiment to make it able to capture the ambivalence of desire.

Repression

If conspiratorial desire is grounded on repression, then repression cannot be described in conventional psychoanalytic terms, at least for the following reasons:

1   Psychoanalysis is focused on apparently irrational phenomena like hysteric symptoms or paranoid delusions, which manifest content hides a latent content. For example, the manifest content of the paranoid delusion that one is secretly persecuted by his doctor can be explained by the latent content of a repressed desire. In contrast, conspiracy theories are apparently rational because their manifest contents consist of reasoning, but the reasoning nevertheless brings a latent gratification (Adorno 1994, 53–54, 2000, 54).

2 In psychoanalysis, the unconscious is structured by the Oedipal complex. In contrast, the latent content of conspiracy theories, like the unconscious of popular culture in general, recognizes taboos only partially, and often only in order to transgress them (Adorno 1994, 54). Because of that, rather than stemming from an originary trauma, the latent content is more like a tree of trees grafted onto each other without a central root or a stalk (Freud 1962, 195), and in that sense, it is rhizomatic (Deleuze and Guattari 1987, 7–13).

3 The work of the unconscious consists of the representation of latent content through processes like condensation and displacement. But in the case of conspiracy theories, as with other seemingly irrational phenomena of popular culture, the latent content is represented on the level of manifest content by innuendos, phrases with floating significance like 'you know what I mean,' suspension of the pragmatic conventions of serious speech acts, and blurring of the boundary between fact and fiction (Adorno 1994, 53–54, 68, 2000, 19).

4 The unconscious of popular culture is sanitized because popular culture tries to avoid the dangers of fulfillment of latent desires by endless deferral. In that sense, the consumers of popular culture, including conspiracy theorists, are like customers who, instead of dining in a restaurant, are trying to derive pleasure from reading the menu in order to contain anxiety about not being unreasonable (Horkheimer and Adorno 2002, 111).

5 The psychoanalytic unconscious is individual. Since the unconscious of popular culture is sanitized, it consists of series of socially acceptable transgressions that can be developed into merchandise, sold and consumed at a mass scale as any other product of the dream factories of late capitalism (Adorno 1994, 67–8).

Theodor Adorno hoped to capture the specific features of repression in popular culture by the concept of bi-phasic syndrome, briefly discussed in the previous chapter in the context of social suffering (Adorno 1994, 89–96).

The concept was introduced to psychoanalysis by Otto Fenichel to describe a type of compulsive behavior composed of two acts (2014, 270–2). The first component is an act of transgression, and it is often imaginary. The second act represents a negation of the first. Imagine for example a subject who misbehaves and then punishes herself for her misbehavior. Fenichel believed that the symptom functioned as a defense mechanism which allowed the subject both to enjoy her transgression and to evade the guilt of it.

In order to make Fenichel's concept applicable to popular culture, Adorno reformulated it along the following lines:

1 The defense mechanism described by Fenichel can be employed in any situation in which one needs to dissolve a contradiction, and because of

that, the syndrome has spread in late modern societies as irresistibly as bureaucratic rationality (Adorno 1994, 105).

2   The functions of the syndrome are not limited to assuaging guilt, and they often include evasion of responsibility or mitigation of an unbearable situation (Adorno 1994, 154).

3   The behavior of the subject can be only mildly compulsive, such as the impulse to check your daily horoscope (Adorno 1994, 87).

4   The sequence of the act is reversible, as for example when, after suffering through another day of work, one would compensate for it by indulging in some reasonable luxury or some modest transgression (Adorno 1994, 100–1).

The reformulated concept of bi-phasic syndrome seemed able to describe the distinguishing features of many apparently irrational phenomena of popular culture, including conspiracy theories (Adorno 1994, 154). However, if such phenomena differed from the phenomena studied by psychoanalysis not only in their severity but also in their mechanism, then conspiracy theorists should not be identified with paranoiacs. Therefore, Adorno tried to distinguish between them by his concept of paranoid personality.[7]

In order to understand the difference made by the concept of paranoid personality, let us briefly compare its mechanism with the delirium of persecution discussed by Freud in the context of the case of President Schreber (Freud 1958, 40). From a psychoanalytic perspective, delirium of persecution is a product of at least the following operations. In principle, desire works by being invested in objects. The latent content of a delirium of persecution is produced by investment of desire in a significant other, like Schreber's brother. The desire is repressed because the subject experiences it as a threat. The manifest content of the delirium is generated by the operations of projection and inversion; the first projects the threatening desire as an external threat, and the second inverts the value of the other from positive to negative. Of course, the manifest content of the delirium can be also shaped by other unconscious operations, for instance by a metaphoric substitution of another person associated by some resemblance with the originary object of desire, like the substitution of Dr. Flechsig for Schreber's brother. The delirium can also involve metonymic displacement of desire from one object to another on the basis of some contiguity.

In contrast, in the case of conspiracy theories, the latent content is not fully repressed. As we have already said, it is both represented and neutralized at the level of the manifest content by gestures or common-sense phrases which mark it off as non-serious. And because of the implosion of the latent in the manifest content, in the case of conspiracy theories, the unconscious projections, inversions, or substitutions do not bring about a transition from positive to negative value and from internal to external threat; rather, they bring forth a constant oscillation. In effect, the disjunctive logic of the unconscious operations characteristic of the delirium of persecution is transformed into conjunctive logic. In other words, the 'either . . . or . . . ' characteristic of the psychoanalytic unconscious turns into 'and . . . and then . . . ' (Deleuze and Guattari 1983, 5), as if popular conspiracy theories short-circuit the mechanism of paranoia in order to make it produce a pulsation rather than a condition.

The concept developed by Adorno provided the ground for the diagnostics of paranoid personality in the next decades – it was introduced in DSM-I (1952, 34) and retained in the next editions of the canonical manual (DSM-II 1968, 42; DSM-III 1980, 307–9).

More importantly, the concept of paranoid personality provided the ground for the concept of paranoid style introduced by Richard Hofstadter (1996), which shaped research on conspiracy theories until the 1980s, of course, together with the very concept of conspiracy theory proposed by Karl Popper (1966, 1962; Knight and Butter 2016).

However, the concept of paranoid personality is grounded on the work of desire, which does not hide inside the subject. As we have already said, conspiratorial desire has been reified as a product of industry, sold as entertainment, and consumed as the subliminal messages that shape our free time, and if it is unconscious, it is an externalized and socialized unconscious (Adorno 1994, 51–4).[8]

How is an externalized and socialized unconscious possible? Let us take messages like 'you have a chance' or 'you have a choice' (Horkheimer and Adorno 2002, 117–18). Such messages operate like advertising, the floating signifiers of which work even if we are distracted. Indeed, is not any story of a felicitous success against all odds also a message that we have a chance, and does not any TV guide communicate to us that we have a choice? The unconscious of popular culture is triangulated by latent messages of that type, by seen but unnoticed messages which constitute us as subjects of chance and choice, and therefore as subjects responsible for their past choices and their lost chances.

Perhaps, in order to distinguish this type of socially produced and consumed latent messages from the repressed content in psychoanalysis, we should call them subliminal (Adorno 1994, 169). But if the work of desire in popular culture depends on the articulation of subliminal messages, then it is an effect of communication.

Subliminal messages

What subliminal messages organize conspiratorial desire?

In the fall of 2002, the lower house of the Russian parliament discussed a motion for resolution which appealed to President Vladimir Putin to take measures against the geophysical weapon supposedly developed by the United States (Duma 2002).

The bill claimed that the High-Frequency Active Aurorial Research Program (HAARP), funded by the Air Force, the Navy, and the Defense Advanced Research Projects Agency of the United States, had reached the stage at which it could turn the Earth itself into a weapon, triggering a revolution in military technology comparable to the weaponization of powder.

The motion for resolution was introduced by the deputy chair of the parliamentary committee on information policy, Tatyana Astrakhankina. The first question asked after her introductory speech was about the nature of her sources. Astrakhankina explained that the relevant information was collected from open American sources because there were not any closed American or Russian sources relevant to the topic.

It seems that one of the sources was a paper by Michel Chossudovsky, a professor of economics at the University of Ottawa (2001). Chossudovsky had already acquired some reputation as an anti-establishment intellectual, and the local newspaper even compared him to Chomsky on account of his studies on the globalization of poverty (O'Neill 1998). In 2001, he established a Centre for Research on Globalization based in Montreal whose mission was to provide information about the new world order (Global Research 2018), to support social justice and world peace, and to continue in the footsteps of his father (Chossudovsky 2006). The Center is currently supporting a website with mirrors in seven languages, online videos and a YouTube channel, and a radio show; the site is currently among the top 6,000 in the United States and among the top 14,000 websites globally (Global Research 2018).[9]

Chossudovsky accused the United States government of intentionally concealing the potential military applications of HAARP, which could use "induced ionospheric modifications" to manipulate the climate, water resources, tectonic processes, and the agriculture of the targeted countries, as well as the mental functioning of their populations. Chossudovsky believed that HAARP signaled the coming of a new type of war based on weaponizing the economy, and in effect his paper reproduced the latent message that we were exposed to risks that we would be soon unable to control, but we still had a chance as long as we acted now (Chossudovsky 2001).[10]

To support the claim, Chossudovsky referred to an allegedly prophetic phrase about weather modification by Zbigniew Brzezinski, as well as to scattered statements by scientists, politicians, and military officers. He also cited the Motion for Resolution A4–0005/99 on the dangers of HAARP at the Committee on Foreign Affairs of the European Parliament in 1999, which did not attract much public attention. Still, Chossudovsky's claim was not better justified than the papers about a vaccine conspiracy published by his research center (Child Health Safety 2012). Russian mainstream scientists often cited vaccine conspiracy theories as an illustration of the dangers of pseudo-science (Aleksandrov 2017), and yet the 2002 motion for resolution was drafted by a working group which included three renowned mainstream scientists. Why did they find Chossudovsky's theory about HAARP plausible?

After answering the question about her sources, Astrakhankina gave the floor to Yuri Perunov, a leading figure in the Central Research Institute of Engineering and an author of numerous patents of invention, to explain in more detail the reliability of the information. Perunov, a doctor of technical sciences, immediately voiced his reservations about the media sources on the program. But then, papers like the one by Chossudovsky did not claim full or reliable knowledge. They claimed only limited and uncertain knowledge enough to ask the question 'what if.'

'What if the environment could be weaponized?' was a counterfactual question, so it could not be answered by facts. Moreover, it was a question about risks, and to claim that the weaponization of the environment was beyond question meant to claim that it was impossible. Yet such a counterclaim would be untenable itself because, even if the risks were infinitesimally small, they could never reach the zero of pure impossibility, and even a remote probability of transforming the Earth into a weapon could be disastrous. If one started to question academic credentials instead of addressing such a threatening question, would not it seem that one was just trying to evade it?

Perunov stated before the parliament that if such a weapon had been successfully developed, then it could not be locked onto a specific target; therefore, it could not be controlled, and even its testing could have unpredictable and potentially ruinous consequences which he could explain in more detail to the members of parliament. However, he said, if such a weapon had been really developed, it would soon be too late. Of course, the members of parliament did not want to hear more details, as they got the politically irresistible subliminal message that it was time to take measures.

In the coming months, the debate in the Russian parliament enjoyed intensive coverage on websites like Chossudovsky's Centre for Research on Globalization or in the entertainment sections of less alternative media. The next year, it was cited as a justification for a research project on the potential health effects of HAARP, funded by the Organization for the Advancement of Knowledge[11] (Miller and Miller 2003). Later on, the research project was cited as a sign of academic recognition by a thinker, digital artist, and healer who hoped to counter the detrimental psychobiological effects of HAARP through meditation and art therapy (Miller 2018).

In the context of the endless reverberations of the debate on geophysical weapons in popular culture, its manifest content was washed away. But one can still hear in its echo at least two subliminal messages: an inarticulate need to escape vulnerability and an insatiable demand for security.

Object-cause of desire

Although conspiratorial desire is an effect of communication and resists classical psychoanalysis, it can be described by concepts introduced by Jacques Lacan.

From a Lacanian perspective, the work of desire involves an impossible object-cause. In this section, I will outline it on the basis of the graph of desire (Lacan 2002, 1959, 1958). However, the account will simplify many Lacanian concepts, it will leave out others, and it will not cover the whole graph, let alone the whole Lacanian theory of desire.

As a starting point, let us assume that desire grows from need.

Need often depends on others, and in order to fulfill a need, one has to communicate it. Communicating the need means articulating it by signifiers, but signifiers make sense if they are put in order; for example, the symbolic order of language, but also computer code, tarot cards, or road signs. Yet, notwithstanding their diversity, the different forms of symbolic order share the following features:[12]

1   Any symbolic order is constituted by at least two series of discrete elements. If we take the example of traffic lights, then the first series will consist of the colors red, yellow, and green, and the second series will consist of commands that could be phrased like 'stop,' 'look out,' and 'go.'

2   The symbolic order is composed of signs, but signs are relationships, not entities. For our purposes, the sign can be defined as a relationship of equivalence between elements of the two series which constitute the symbolic order. For example, the red traffic light is a sign as far as it implies an equivalence between the red color and 'stop.'

3   The value of a sign, the space of its possible meanings, is circumscribed by its difference from other signs. For example, the value of 'yellow' is defined by its difference from the other signs in the symbolic order of traffic lights, and it can take different meanings depending on the circumstances, like 'start the engine,' 'slow down,' or even 'speed up because the light will turn red in a moment.'

4   The differences that circumscribe the value of the sign stand out against the background of two other types of relationships. The first type can be called metaphoric relationships, if we conceive of metaphor as a

substitution of one sign for another founded on resemblance (for example, when one says that a project has been given a green light, she is substituting the sign 'green' taken from the code of traffic lights for a sign that belongs to the administrative code like 'permission' or 'approval').

5 In general, we use signs to compose sequences like phrases, narratives, and formulas. The value of the sign stands out as well against the background of its relationships with the preceding or the succeeding signs in the sequence. Since that type of relationship is based on the contiguity between the signs in the sequence, we can call it metonymic if we define metonymy as association of signs based on contiguity (as, for example, the yellow traffic light means 'start the engine' because of its contiguity with the preceding red light and the subsequent green light).

6 In order to take into account that signs have a dual composition, let us call their two components signifier and signified, for example a green light and 'go,' and let us assume that the signified functions as the meaning of the signifier. As we have already said, the signifier and the signified are equivalent, and because of that, the relation between the signifier and the signified is reversible. Imagine for example a picture of green traffic light with the caption 'go.' In that case, 'go' would function as a signifier and the green light as a signified. However, since the relation between the signifier and the signified is reversible, they differ in function rather than in substance.

7 The signifieds and the signifiers are not perfectly superimposed. Take for example the phrase 'I would rather. . . . ' Its meaning depends on what comes next. And since the meaning of a sequence of signifiers is its signified, the signified is sliding beneath the signifier toward what comes next. In order to stop this sliding away, one has to fix the signified. But this is possible only if the sequence of signifiers comes to a stop, if some form of punctuation marks its end (we can call such punctuation anchoring points; Lacan 1993, 268). Now, imagine that our phrase stops at a negation: 'I would rather not.' The negation will reverse the meaning of the sequence of signifiers 'I would rather,' but the reversal will come after some delay, so the signified will be fixed retroactively. However, the signified is also what the speaking subject wants or needs to say. So, the anchoring point will inscribe retroactively in the chain of signifiers the intention of the speaking subject by associating it with a signified. If we take into account that signifieds differ from signifiers only in function, then the anchoring point will fix the meaning of the sequence by ascribing to some signifiers the function of signifieds, i.e. the function to represent the subject to other signifiers (Lacan 2002, 693–4).

Let us turn back to desire. As it was already said, to communicate a need, one needs to inscribe it in the symbolic order. But the symbolic order is not the subject of need; it is another. Of course, it is not a real other like the people with whom we communicate in our daily lives. But it is still the necessary condition without which we cannot communicate with any real others. Since it is important to distinguish the otherness of the symbolic other from the real others, let us call it the Other.

Now, need can be inscribed in the symbolic order if it is articulated as a demand. Demands are normally addressed to real others, but they can be communicated to those real others only through the symbolic order, so the demands are also addressed to the Other. And since the Other is abstract, any demand has an abstract dimension in which it is essentially a demand for love, a demand for the desire of the Other. Lacan claimed that the abstract dimension of demands can be captured by the question '*che vuoi*,' 'What do you want?'

The question 'What do you want?' cannot be answered by need because questions are articulated in the symbolic order and need belongs to the order of the real. It cannot be reduced to demand, either, because it is not a question of the type 'What do I want?' It is a question about the desire of the Other. So, it can be answered only from the position of the Other, which is inaccessible to the subject. Since the question 'What do you want?' cannot be reduced to demand or need, it opens up a space beyond them that can be easily discerned in cases in which one demands what one does not need, or one feels need despite one's demands being met (Lacan 1958, 79). That gap between demand and need is the space of desire.

So, desire is constituted by the question of the desire of the Other. But the Other of the symbolic order is silent, just as language does not speak itself, although it enables us to speak. Because of that, the question 'What do you want?' is enigmatic; it is inherently open. Since what is desired by the subject depends on that question, the object that causes her desire is open as well. Therefore, it is constituted by a void, and it is precisely this lack that causes desire. In consequence, the object-cause of desire cannot be reduced to a real or symbolic object, and it cannot be attained even if the relevant demands are fulfilled. In that sense, it is the difference between the real need and its symbolic articulation as a demand.[13] Because of that, the object which causes desire can be described as a remainder of the real within the symbolic order. And since such a remainder is real, it can be represented only by signifiers associated with it on the basis of some contiguity. Of course, any isolated signifier would unavoidably misrepresent desire because it would fail to signify the lacking object-cause. To capture this lack, the signifiers are composed in a metonymic chain in which the endless displacement of one signifier of desire by another will signify the incessant sliding away of its object-cause.

Now, since the object-cause of desire is lacking, then the desire of the Other should also be caused by a lack. But if the symbolic order is punctuated by a lack, then it would be inconsistent, which would threaten the very possibility of recognition of desire. So, in order not to give way as to her desire, i.e., in order to maintain desire, the subject has to cover up the double lack of the object-cause of her desire and of the object-cause of the desire of the Other. At the same time, the subject should sustain the double lack because the lack of this constitutive lack would transform desire into anxiety (Lacan 1963, 35).

The subject usually tries to follow the self-contradictory imperative of both sustaining and covering up the lacking object which causes desire by articulating a fantasy, an imaginary scene that answers the question what the Other wants through staging the impossible relation of the subject to the object-cause of desire (Žižek 1992, 6).

The fantasy of saving the world

To speak before the Russian parliament about geophysical weapons certainly involved desire. But what was the object which caused that desire?

Astrakhankina demanded that the Russian president work for an internationally imposed ban on experiments with geophysical weapons, initiate a global convention limiting the number, localization, and power of systems similar to HAARP, and demand the development of relevant international legislation under the auspices of the United Nations.

But was that really necessary, particularly in view of the fact that the threat of geophysical weapons seemed somewhat speculative and the Defense Minister just addressed the parliament about the countless vulnerabilities and inadequacies of the Russian military forces? Should we really ask the president to concern himself with that, asked one of the members of the parliament, as if he had nothing to do?

Astrakhankina justified her demand not only by reference to risks or information sources. In response to one of the questions, she described the following scenario: the Russian president would call the president of the United States to let him know that he knows about HAARP, and then Russia would put the issue on the agenda of the UN Security Council; all the world's presidents or prime ministers, shocked by the potential risks, would then start nationally funded independent research projects, and on the basis of the findings, the UN General Assembly would then make the Security Council develop appropriate international legislation. That was certainly a fantastic scenario: the Russian president would fill in the lack suffered by humanity – perhaps the lack of sustainable global order, or the lack of global equality, or the lack of responsible leadership – and Astrakhankina would fill in the lack of awareness in the president.

But then, what was actually lacking?

Astrakhankina's scenario did not articulate the lack of an object which could be defined or even identified. The object of her demand would lack only if the geophysical weapon started to unmake the world; it would become an object only after the loss of the symbolic order itself. So, in trying to make sense of the demand, her parliamentary colleagues, those laic analysts, started to search for the hidden object, which caused her demand, the real object of her desire.

One of the speakers claimed that Astrakhankina was involved in a secret plan of the Communist Party to destroy the great country of the United States by hindering scientific progress, just like it destroyed the great country of the Soviet Union after 1989. Another speaker speculated that the actual cause of Astrakhankina's demand was that she wanted to use the media coverage to insinuate that the president lacked the knowledge necessary to protect the country, that the government was impotent, and hence that the communists could run the country better. Yet another speaker referred to her overambitious character and to her declining political career (indeed, she had recently left the Communist Party to join an even more marginal group in the parliament, the agricultural faction).

But any attempt to define Astrakhankina's desire substituted other signifiers for the impossible object of her fantasy. Of course, the substitutions were not just acts of discursive violence; they were motivated by some contiguity between her demand and the substituted signifiers, for example her former affiliation or political positions. Because of that, the substituted signifiers functioned as metonymies of the object of desire that caused her demand and invited other substitutions.

Although the object which caused the debate – the ultimate power over the real, the real power that escaped the symbolic order – was lacking, it brought forth a chain of metonymies, indeed a web of metonymies rapidly developing beyond any intention, an overflow of desire.

Symbolic power

How does conspiratorial desire work?

In order to understand this, we need to take into account that the symbolic order is an instance of power.

Let us turn once more to the example of Gelb-Goldstein color sorting test, discussed in the first chapter. The subject of the test is asked to sort out a heap of colored wool skeins. For the sake of this argument, let us assume that the skeins form a layer of visible matter.[14] To order it, the subject has to differentiate the matter into individual elements and put the elements in their places, which are organized as a web of distances and proximities associated with functions and developed in open series. In other words, the subject needs to impose on the layer of visible matter a layer of visible forms and in that sense to compose the plane of the visible.

Again, this is a test for color anomia. The anomic subject shows herself because she constantly reorders the skeins, but the constant reordering does not mean that she is unable to order. On the contrary; she is relentlessly covering the visible matter of the skeins with layers of forms. The subject is anomic not because she cannot put the skeins in order but because she cannot stop, because the order she produces is fluid and the forms she invents are incessantly becoming other. In order to stop her work, she needs an order that is detached from the fluidity of the visible matter, an abstract order that remains stable even if things change. She can do that by superimposing over the plane of the visible the plane of the sayable, the abstract grid of symbolic order.

Imagine that the psychologist asks the subject why she has ordered the skeins like this. A normal subject would explain the order by phrases composed of signifiers that would make sense because they were organized in a symbolic order, i.e. in a plane of the sayable. The anomic subject, on the other hand, will be unable to make sense of the visible order because she will fail to attach the visible to the sayable, and in effect she will not be able to answer the question 'why' asked by the psychologist, as well as the questions 'why' she asks herself, so she will keep reordering the skeins in a desperate effort to capture the fluidity of matter.

In seeing that she is unable to answer the question, the psychologist will probably diagnose her with color anomia. The diagnosis will reinscribe in the symbolic order her inability to make sense of the visible, although under the sign of a disorder. In consequence, she will be involved not only in a play of signifiers but also in a play of forces, which will trigger an intervention of healthcare institutions, insurance companies, governmental agencies, and non-governmental organizations that will produce a flow of capital and knowledge, although perhaps a small amount, an intervention in the plane of the visible.

The layers of the visible and the sayable are not isolated; they form a complex geology of intermediary strata which are not perfectly superimposed on each other but unavoidably produce tension (Deleuze 1988, 38–9). That tension will thrust the subject into her place, and if she does not interiorize it as an intention of recognizing and healing her disorder, if she resists it, then she will have to fight the powerful apparatuses that enforce symbolic order, apparatuses of power intended to subject her to her own good. And, of course, if she will not learn how to make sense of her resistance to the symbolic order, the resistance will be once again reinscribed in the symbolic order by means of an appropriate category, for example delirium of protest.

However, the power of symbolic order is not reducible to power apparatuses like the clinic or the school. Such apparatuses enforce its power because it is powerful. The power of symbolic order rather depends on its efficiency (Žižek 1999, 330–1, 2007, 329–30). Devoid of symbolic efficiency, it would be unable to act; it would be nothing but words; it would be impotent (Žižek 1997).

Yet, in order to be efficient, the symbolic order should transgress the plane of the sayable; it has to become more than words. But how is that possible, if it is composed of words?

Imagine a young girl involved in an embarrassing relationship.[15] In one of her days of passion, while she is walking together with her unlikely knight, she suddenly realizes that her father is looking at her. In her younger days, her desire was staged as a fantasy to be what the father was lacking, and the father is still so significant to her that in the context of this example, we can assume that he performs the function of the Other. Now, the look of the father says 'no.' The father denies his recognition of a relationship that is unassimilable to her place in the symbolic order, inconsistent neither with the part of a good daughter prescribed to her by her place nor with her future share as a good bourgeois wife. But, since the father looks at her through the grid of the social order, he does not see the object of her desire.

We have already assumed that the object-cause of desire is constituted by a lack, but that does not mean just that something is lacking. The object-cause of desire is a lack of being (Lacan 1988, 223), and in that sense it is lost from the origin. Yet what is the originary loss constitutive of that object? Let us assume that it is a loss of jouissance, i.e. enjoyment that is so intense that it is impossible to bear, and because of that it is associated with death and grounded on one of the principles of organization of the psychic apparatus, the death drive.[16] That impossible enjoyment is lost because it is associated with the infantile experience of imaginary unity with the Other foreclosed by the symbolic order, a remnant of which is the object-cause of desire, discussed in a previous section (although the object-cause of desire constitutes as an object the loss of enjoyment rather than being the enjoyment itself).

In the context of our example, the concept of jouissance is important because it explains why the girl cannot just give way to her desire. From a psychoanalytic perspective, desire is a vital power and its depletion would amount to subjective destitution, a life of poverty from the inside, the subject of which does not merely have nothing: she even has nothing to desire (Lacan 1967, 6; Žižek 1992, 198).

So the girl is caught in a double bind. On one hand, she cannot give way to the object-cause of her desire. On the other hand, the eyes of the father are saying 'no' to her enjoyment. How can she resolve this double bind?

Imagine that in response she says 'no' to the father. In that case, she would claim that the father is blind to her. But the father performs the function of the symbolic order, and if the symbolic order was unable to capture something, if it lacked something, if it was fractured by a lack, then it would be inconsistent. As we have already seen, that would threaten the very possibility of communication with others. Of course, she could evade this threat by dissociating the father from the symbolic order, perhaps as an imposter or a deceiver. But as far as the symbolic order is an instance of desire, it is constituted by a lack, and her fantasy of being the object of her father's desire has covered the lack in the symbolic order as a screen on which she imagined the scene of her desire, as if it was a film scene frozen just before a traumatic event. Because of that, to relegate the father from his symbolic function, to erase him from her fantasy, would mean to slide into the trauma from which she protected herself by the frozen scenario of her desire, to open the lack in the symbolic order covered by the screen of her fantasy.

But now imagine that in response, the girl is suddenly passing into act; for example, that she falls on a nearby railway track. That is certainly an act, and it is an act of significance. Yet it does not refer to other signifiers in the symbolic order. Its significance consists of what caused the girl to pass into act; it signifies its cause, but since the cause is not integrated in the symbolic order, it is unknown and cannot be known. So, passing into act signifies an unknown cause which lies beyond the symbolic order. But then the act on one hand belongs to the symbolic order, as any signification, and on the other hand it passes beyond the symbolic order. In that sense, it is a transgressive act.

Such a transgressive act has at least two important effects. Firstly, it has the significance of saying 'no' to the situation, which threatens to fracture the screen of fantasy. Yet saying 'no' to the threat means saying 'yes' to the fantasy and the symbolic order in which it is inscribed. Therefore, it also means saying 'yes' to her place in the symbolic order, to her part as a good daughter, to her share of a future as a good wife, to her image in the eyes of the father. But, secondly, saying 'yes' to her place in the symbolic order means saying 'no' to the object-cause of her desire, and not as if in her suicidal act she has finally come to her senses and decided to choose a more appropriate object of desire. It is rather as if the object-cause of her desire has always been nothing, as if she is now facing the question of how she could ever desire such nothingness – an impossible question about an impossible object that has always already been lacking, the very threshold of melancholia (Butler 1997, 170–4). In that sense, saying 'no' to the object which caused her desire means excluding it from the symbolic order as a meaningless remnant. But an object excluded from the symbolic order does not disappear. Since there is nothing sayable about it, it is relegated to the plane of the visible. Therefore, passing into act articulates the object which caused her desire as a real residue, as flesh, which is cut off from the symbolic order and falls down as her body. The double effect of such passage into act can be illustrated by the following story:

> Take the angry response of Groucho Marx when caught in a lie: 'Whom do you believe, your eyes or my words?' This apparently absurd logic renders perfectly the functioning of the symbolic order, in which the symbolic mask-mandate matters more than the direct reality of the individual who wears this mask and/or assumes this mandate.
>
> (Žižek 2007, 328)

Passing into act splits the visible from the sayable in order to uphold the symbolic efficiency of the sayable, in order to guarantee the power of the symbolic order. It cuts off the visible as a meaningless remnant which in effect takes the function of the real cause, which makes one fall from her place in the symbolic order or, to put it otherwise, draws one in the fall.

In sum, symbolic order is efficient if it produces such passages into act, if it is able to effect transgressive acts that affirm it and at the same time articulate real remnants from the sayable which are meaningless yet cause desire.

But what if the symbolic order becomes inefficient, if its power is depleted?

Slavoj Žižek has claimed that this is one of the characteristic features of late modernity:

> A wide scope of phenomena the resurgent ethico/religious "fundamentalisms" which advocate a return to the Christian or Islamic patriarchal division of sexual roles; the New Age massive re-sexualization of the universe, i.e., the return to pre-modern, pagan, sexualized cosmo-ontology; the growth of "conspiracy theories" as a form of popular "cognitive mapping" seem to counter the retreat of the big Other. These phenomena cannot be simply dismissed as "regressive" . . . . Rather, these disturbing phenomena compel us to elaborate the contours of the big Other's retreat: The paradoxical result of this mutation in the "inexistence of the Other" (of the growing collapse of the symbolic efficiency) is precisely the re-emergence of the different facets of a big Other which exists effectively, in the Real, and not merely as symbolic fiction.
>
> (Žižek 1997)

Conspiratorial desire can be explained as one of the popular mechanisms that are supposed to repair the depleting power of symbolic order

(Žižek 1997, 1992, 250). Conspiracy theorists do that by positing a latent order beneath the manifest symbolic order, an Other of the Other that escapes its impotence. But it is impossible to articulate an Other of the Other, because then the second-order Other would be lacking in the symbolic order; the symbolic order would be inconsistent, and it could signify nothing but a disorder (Lacan 2002, 688). Therefore, this second-order Other can be posited only in the real, as the unknown cause of an act of transgression (Žižek 1997).[17]

But then conspiracy theories are not just counterproductive reasoning, they are *passage déraisonnable à l'acte*, the passing of reason into an unreasonable act.

The real of politics

If conspiracy theories are a form of passing into act, then they should produce a material remnant from the symbolic order, like the body falling on the railway track in the example discussed in the previous section. But conspiracy theories rarely lead to such a downfall. What, then, is their material remnant?

The parliamentary debate on geophysical weapons unfolded before the eyes of a silent majority – the president's party, which never went so far as to doubt the social order.

The motion for resolution failed because, although there were almost no votes against it, the silent majority of those who identified themselves with the established order prevailed, as usual (55.6% did not vote, 41.8% voted in favor of the motion, 2% voted against; Duma 2002).

In effect, the debate on the potential weaponization of the environment unfolding before their silent eyes produced mostly sound and fury. The reactions brought forth by Astrakhankina's speech were recorded in the minutes as "noise," and the voices kept on getting louder. "I deeply respect you, but you do not know what you are talking about," said one of the parliament members. "You should apologize to the lady," responded a loyal colleague from the faction of the parliamentary agriculturalists. Then came the question of who owed apology to whom, which soon overshadowed the question of geophysical warfare, a far more abstract problem. But there was also the question who had the right to speak and when, and what was the relevant parliamentary procedure. Noise.

And although that noise was a meaningless remnant cut off from the symbolic order of the parliamentary proceedings, although it was marked as a loss of sense even in the parliamentary minutes, it articulated an incomprehensible desire to speak indicating causes which seemed unknown even to the speakers themselves. "Idiots do not disappear, they only evolve," explained one speaker to another. Indeed, what could have caused a response like that?

But if passing into act covers the lack in the symbolic order through meaningless remnants in the real, was the noise such a remnant?[18] Was the act of speaking amid the parliamentary noise, before the silent eyes of the party that was going to govern for the future decade, passing into act? Or was it just acting out, an ostentatious behavior oriented at the Other (Lacan 1963, 109)?

If acting out differs from passing into act because the latter articulates a cause of desire unknown to the subject, how could one expect the speakers to know what desire drove their countless 'you must' or 'you should not have' statements, or the endless pleas of excuses, or the always-relevant arguments about technicalities?

On the other hand, what if parliamentary democracy, faced with the incalculable risks of late modernity, has become a mode of passing into act?

Social order

Conspiracy theories also respond to the impossible imperative of desire by staging a fantasy.[19] However, the conspiratorial fantasy is different from the structure of fantasies described in the previous sections.

From a psychoanalytic perspective, fantasy is defined by its function rather than by its content (Glynos 2001, 202). For example, in the previously discussed case of Sidonie, the young girl in an embarrassing relationship, the fantasy has the function of a screen on which she stages the impossible object of her desire and which covers the lack in the symbolic order.

Conspiratorial fantasies are also screens covering the lack in the symbolic order, but they stage impossibly undesirable objects. In order to explain how, we need at least two more concepts: the concepts of empty signifier and hegemony.

Empty signifier

An empty signifier is a signifier lacking a signified (Laclau 1996, 37). A signifier is a relational concept, and it is meaningless if it is detached from the relationship of asymmetric equivalence between signifier and signified. Therefore, the concept of empty signifier is meaningful only if we assume that it signifies a lack.

Yet lacks can be different. Take for example indexical expressions. The meaning of 'I,' 'here,' or 'now' is contingent on the subject of the statement, and if it is abstracted from any particular subject, then it signifies a lack that any speaking body can fill. Let us call that type of signifier a floating signifier (Laclau 1996, 36, 2002, 131).[20]

However, we should distinguish another type of signifier that signifies a lack in the symbolic order. To explain that, let us turn once again to the Gelb-Goldstein color sorting test. Imagine that the frustrated subject of the test finally bursts out and asks the psychologist, 'What do you want from me?' The psychologist coldly responds, 'I want you to order the wool skeins by color.' Now, 'order' is certainly a signifier. But what does it signify? On one hand, it refers to what is lacking in the work of the anomic subject. Yet, on the other hand, it refers to what is needed if her work is supposed to make sense. Therefore, 'order' signifies a lack that is both impossible and necessary to fill, and in that sense it is an empty signifier in the proper sense (Laclau 1991, 27; Stavrakakis 2002, 80).

Hegemony

Social order is composed of social relations, but social relations are not merely visible. They are of significance as far as they are articulated as signifiers (Laclau 2002, 68).

Take for example the concept of the people. Although this covers a visible mass of bodies, its identity depends not on the identity of the bodies but on the representation of a border that divides the people from their other, let us say the elites, and demarcates a virtual space shared by anybody who is different from the elites. In that sense, the concept articulates a chain of equivalence between different bodies. It is this chain of equivalence that constitutes the people as a body politic, rather than the endlessly disseminating web of proximities and distances between the visible bodies[21] (Laclau 2002, 131, 160–1).

Therefore, social order is symbolic order, and the identity of any element of the social order is defined by its difference from other elements which can be substituted for it or stand in some contiguity to it (Laclau 2002, 68).

But the social order is a totality, and the significance of any social action or interaction is grounded on it as a totality, just like language as a totality is the condition of possibility of any meaningful speech act (Laclau 1996, 37).

Since the totality of social order is the ground of any significance, it should also be articulated as a signifier. But signifiers imply difference. If the symbolic order was defined by its difference from something else, its significance would depend on something else and it would not be a totality. So, the constitutive difference should be internal to the social order (Laclau 2002, 69–70, 1996, 38).

Therefore, social order is defined by a remnant that is excluded from it and at the same time is internal to it. But, since this remnant is excluded from the totality of social order, it is in an equivalent relation to any of its elements. Because of that, this constitutive remnant can be represented by any element of the order (Laclau 2002, 70), and hence, the element that represents it is essentially contingent. What is more, it is inescapably unstable because it is articulated as a tension between the particular identity of the contingent element and its abstract function as a representation of a chain of equivalent relationships of exclusion (Laclau 2002, 130, 1996, 38).

Now, since such a contingent element represents a remnant that is excluded from the social order, its signified is lacking and it functions as an empty signifier (Laclau 2002, 70–1, 1996, 39; Glynos 2001, 201; Stavrakakis 2002, 73).

Furthermore, as the empty signifier of the constitutive other is a contingent element that represents the totality, it produces the powerful effect usually termed hegemony (Laclau 1996, 43; Laclau and Mouffe 1985, 139; Glynos and Howarth 2007, 105–7).[22] For our present purposes, let us assume that hegemony consists of the power to represent what is common and therefore to represent a form of power, the resistance to which is uncommon; in other words, any resistance to this power can be justified only by means of extraordinary political, economic, or cultural capital.

Conspiratorial fantasy

If conspiratorial fantasy is described by the concepts outlined above,[23] then it differs from the general structure of fantasy because it articulates an empty signifier that stands for a lack in the social order and because it produces hegemony by representing the social order as a whole (Glynos 2001, 201–2).

Another important difference from the fantasies discussed in the previous sections is that conspiratorial fantasy is characterized by a negative conditionality, since it represents not the object which causes desire but rather what would have been that object if there was not a conspiracy. It is a fantasy about a stolen or forestalled object-cause of desire, about the loss of the very cause that makes the social order desirable for us – our enjoyment (Žižek 1999, 201, 2018, 172; Stavrakakis 2007, 197).

Because of its negative conditionality, conspiratorial fantasy is articulated as an imaginary scenario of meaningless violence, the function of which is not to cover the constitutive lack of desire by staging the impossible relation between the subject and the object-cause of her desire but rather to reaffirm in the real the power lost because of the impotence of the symbolic order (Žižek 1999, 322–3).

It seems that behind the screen of conspiratorial fantasy that tries to hold together the symbolic order despite its fractured power, behind the endlessly developing scenario of frames of meaningless violence, frozen just before the time of living on, just before the time after the trauma, we can discern the outlines of the proper object of conspiracy theories: the political monster.

Political leadership

The hegemonic effect of empty signifiers can be recognized by the advantage they bring in political competition.

The most vocal opponent of the movement for resolution on the geophysical weapon allegedly developed by the United States was Vladimir Zhirinovsky, a self-proclaimed nationalistic liberal democrat who was often considered the most recognizable Russian right-wing populist.

It was Zhirinovsky who claimed that the motion for resolution was a surreptitious communist plot to hinder progress and ultimately to destroy the United States, a happy country where "nobody smokes, all have an average income of 3000 USD, and anybody can immediately get a house, a car, a washing machine, and excellent services, a country without poor or beggars" (Duma 2002).

Although Zhirinovsky's argument did not make much sense on the level of its manifest content, it performed at least the following discursive operations:

1 The argument amassed contingent signifiers like the United States, the Soviet Union, the Russian tsar, the millions of young mobsters or hustlers who could seize power at any minute, and the research group of Academic Selyakov, which had developed a project to make Russia five times richer and stronger.
2 The accumulation of signifiers foregrounded a double equivalence between them – enjoyment of power and the threat to enjoyment posed by a hostile other, which figure was circumscribed by a double opposition between 'us' and 'them' – 'us, the Russians' versus 'them, the other nations,' but also 'us, the Russians whose enjoyment of power was stolen' versus 'them, the communists who stole it.'
3 Zhirinovsky tried to identify Astrakhankina with the communists who stole power, and since he opposed her, the argument was intended to make 'us' identify 'ourselves' with him, and in that sense to pose him as the political actor who protects the enjoyment of power, hence as the actor who would be able to restore it, who could fill in the lack of power, whose absence would amount to further loss of power.

In sum, Zhirinovsky used his conspiracy theory to articulate himself as an empty signifier of order, as the signifier of a leader capable of compensating for the impotence of government. And even though Zhirinovsky was recognized as that empty signifier only contingently, mostly by himself, he managed to represent a lack in the political order that would be soon filled by a master.

Astrakhankina responded with some irony that she was happy to inspire Zhirinovsky for such a passionate speech. But her ironic reference to his improper passion did not provide an alternative articulation of the empty signifier of the leader, and she seemed unable to oppose Zhirinovsky. In effect, although her agricultural and communist colleagues stood up for her, she was put in her place and lost her last chance to take the place in politics she was aspiring to.

Revolutions of the weak

If we can sum up the argument of this chapter, it is that conspiracy theories articulate a desire caused by an impossible object and intended to cover a lack of meaning in the social order by an impossible scenario of conspiracy against it.

But then conspiracy theories articulate an impossibility that escapes the social order and yet is constitutive of it, a disorder that gives the ground for social order. In that sense, conspiracy theories are discursive revolutions.

As far as they do not articulate any alternative order, conspiracy theories are weak revolutions. And as far as they do not rise to hegemonic power, they are revolutions of the weak. Perhaps that is the positive core of the concept of ressentiment, the first concept intended to capture the desire that we now commonly associate with conspiracy theories – the revolution of the weak as weak, the revolution of the slaves as slaves (Deleuze 2005, 109).

But any revolution is a reversal of power relationships (Foucault 1997, 123), and any reversal of power relationships requires more power, just as any resistance to power requires power. Then how is a revolution of the weak as weak possible?

Notes

1 For a powerful critique of contextual explanations of conspiracy theories, see Bratich 2008, 19. For a critique of the concept of conspiracy theories as "cry and rage from the margins," see Fenster 1999, 83.

2 For another version of the history of the concept of paranoia in relation to the concept of conspiracy theory, which describes it as an amalgamation of a delirium of protest, delirium of interpretation, delusion of grandeur, and persecution complex, see Boltanski 2014, 173–7. The version in this book is focused on the problem of counterproductive work of reason rather than on medicalization of suspicion. It does not take into account many variations of the relevant psychiatric arguments and concepts, for which see Shorter 2005, 206–11.

3 On the deviation of monomaniacs from their social position, which shaped the psychiatric problematizations of paranoia, see Esquirol 1845, 320; Boltanski 2014, 175–6.

4 An alternative line of problematization used the concept of delirium of interpretation (Sérieux and Capgras 2008, 448). An important defining feature of this concept was that the subject abused the facts in order to develop a line of thought which would transform them into knowledge about herself.

5 In a paper intended to capture the logic of conspiracy theories, Marc Angenot proposed that ressentiment is the mechanism of conspiratorial reasoning and that they are actually one phenomenon (Angenot 2013, 13).

6 For important comments on the link between conspiracy theories and the repression hypothesis, see Wacquant 2009, 29; Melley 2012, 8.

7 The concept of paranoid personality developed by Adorno was grounded on the concept of psychological type introduced by Ernst Kretschmer and on the political typology developed by Harold Lasswell. The critiques that the concept of paranoia is applicable to conspiracy theories only by analogy or as a metaphor, although convincing in general, often do not take into account its difference from the concept of paranoid personality. See, for example, Knight 2000, 15–19; Fenster 1999, 36; Boltanski 2014, 171–9. For an alternative problematization of conspiracy theories as mass hysteria epidemics, which however fails to provide a convincing explanation of how hysteria can turn into a contagious disease, see Showalter 1997, 11–14.

8 For an argument that conspiracy theories are shaped after late capitalist media spectacles which articulate systematically the fantasy of a central point of control, see Hardt and Negri 2001, 323.

9 For a detailed analysis of Chossudovsky's theory about 9/11, see Knight 2008.

10 Clare Birchall has argued that conspiracy theories make sense of events by problematizing them from the perspective of the future trauma of the worst to come, a line of problematization shared by late modern security apparatuses (Birchall 2006, 62).

11 The Organization for the Advancement of Knowledge is a Seattle-based nongovernmental research institute with a sort of New Age profile.

12 The features are described on the basis of Barthes 1967. The traffic lights example is adapted from Eco 1976, 127–9.

13 On the difference between demand and need in the context of conspiracy theories, see Fenster 1999, 100. On the detail as an object-cause of desire in conspiracy theories, see Fenster 1999, 105–6.

14 The concepts of the visible and sayable are adapted from Deleuze 1988, 32, 38–9.

15 The example is based on the case of Sidonie, in which context Lacan defines his concept of passage into act, *passage à l'acte* (1963, 97–8, 69, 96–109; Freud 1951). For an analysis into passage into act as an act constitutive of the speaking body, which is the condition of possibility of speech acts, as well as a definition of performance as the unconscious remnant of any performative act, see Felman 2003, 65–7. The interpretation of the concept is based on Žižek 2010, 65, 2012, 209–10, 2001, 28–9.

16 For a relevant discussion of the intensive affects produced by conspiracy theories, tentatively captured by the concept of conspiracy rush, which does not use the concept of jouissance, see Fenster 1999, 110–11.

17 In a Lacanian perspective, the positing of the Other in the real is the distinguishing feature of paranoia Žižek 1992, 216. Yet, unlike paranoiacs, conspiracy theorists counterbalance it with cynicism that resists the symbolic order of any authority,

a cynicism that claims to believe only what it really sees and that claims to obey only the imperative of unconstrained choice, yet at the same time enthusiastically indulges in conspiracy theories (Žižek 2012, 337, 1997, 1v992, 219).

18 On voice as passage into act, see Zizek 1999, 319.

19 On conspiracy theories as an element of the cultural apparatus of the covert sphere, which tries to deal with the contradictions of contemporary democracy by means of articulating fantasies and fictions, see Melley 2012, 5–6.

20 From the perspective of Laclau, unlike indexical expressions, floating signifiers in the social order are underdetermined because they belong to more than one chain of equivalence and refer to more than one empty signifier. For more details, see the discussion of social order in this section.

21 Today, revolutionary politics cannot rely on a subject like the proletariat, which can overpower opponents by its sheer multiplicity. Because of that, many leftists find hope in chains of equivalence, which would amalgamate the particular subjects of dispersed demands into a powerful whole. In practice, however, chains of equivalence often turn out to be empty and fragile. I think that parrhesia, discussed in chapter 3, can provide a more reliable ground for revolutionary politics.

22 For a detailed critique of the relevance of the concept of hegemony developed by Laclau to conspiracy theories, see Butter 2014, 16–19. To summarize the argument, on one hand, the concept implies that political and semiotic representations are indistinguishable, and because of that, it is inapplicable to any opposition to conspiracy theories that does not intend to represent the people; on the other hand, the concept is unable to describe how conspiracy theories misrepresent the real struggles for hegemony by distorting and deflecting their issues and by superimposing identities of the people and their enemies that are often resisted by the social actors.

23 For arguments for the relevance of this concept of fantasy to conspiracy theories, see Melley 2012, 14; Dean 1998, 176.

Bibliography

Adorno, Theodor. 2000. *The Psychological Technique of Martin Luther Thomas' Radio Addresses*. Stanford: Stanford UP

Adorno, Theodor. 1994. *The Stars Down to Earth*. London: Routledge

Aleksandrov, Evgeni. 2017. "Academics Will Fight GMO-Phobia and Anti-Vaccination Dissidents", *Defense of Science* 20: 36–9 [Александров, Евгений. Академики поборются с ГМО-фобией и ВИЧ-диссидентством. *В защите науки*]

Angenot, Marc. 2013. "*The Conspiratorial Mind*: For a Dialectical and Rhetorical History." Accessed 15.11.2016, http://marcangenot.com/wp-content/uploads/2011/12/The_Conspiratorial_Mind.pdf

Barthes, Roland. 1967. *Elements of Semiology*. London: Cape

Birchall, Clare. 2006. *Knowledge Goes Pop*. Oxford: Berg

Boltanski, Luc. 2014. *Mysteries & Conspiracies: Detective Stories, Spy Novels, and the Making of Modern Societies*. Cambridge, MA: Polity

Bratich, Jack. 2008. *Conspiracy Panics: Political Rationality and Popular Culture*. Albany: New York UP

Butler, Judith. 1997. *The Psychic Life of Power: Theories in Subjection*. Stanford: Stanford UP

Butter, Michael. 2014. *Plots, Designs, and Schemes: American Conspiracy Theories from the Puritans to the Present*. Berlin: Walter de Gruyter

Child Health Safety. 2012. "The Vaccine Coverup." *Global Research News*, 14.03.2012, Accessed 24.07.2018, www.globalresearch.ca/the-vaccine-coverup-30-years-of-secret-official-transcripts-show-uk-government-experts-cover-up-vaccine-hazards-to-sell-more-vaccines-and-harm-your-kids/5354241

Chossudovsky, Michel. 2006. "Evgeny Chossudovsky: Writer with a Distinguished UN Career." *Global Research*, 18.01. 2006. Accessed 24.07.2018, https://web.archive.org/web/20121023133046/www.globalresearch.ca/evgeny-chossudovsky-writer-with-a-distinguished-un-career/1955

Chossudovsky, Michel. 2001. "Washington's New World Order Weapons Have the Ability to Trigger Climate Change." *Centre for Research on Globalization*, 04.01.2002, Accessed 24.07.2018, https://archives.globalresearch.ca/articles/CHO201A.html

Dean, Jodi. 1998. *Aliens in America: Conspiracy Cultures from Outerspace to Cyberspace*. Ithaca: Cornell UP

Deleuze, Gilles. 2006. "Desire and Pleasure", in Deleuze, Gilles. *Two Regimes of Madness*, 122–34, New York: Columbia UP

Deleuze, Gilles. 2005. *Nietzsche and Philosophy*. London: Continuum

Deleuze, Gilles. 1988. *Foucault*. Minneapolis: Minnesota UP

Deleuze, Gilles and Félix Guattari. 1987. *A Thousand Plateaus: Capitalism and Schizophrenia*. Minneapolis: Minnesota UP

Deleuze, Gilles and Félix Guattari. 1983. *Anti-Oedipus: Capitalism and Schizophrenia*. Minneapolis: Minnesota UP

DSM-III. 1980. *Diagnostic and Statistical Manual of Mental Disorders. Third Edition*. Washington: APA

DSM-II. 1968. *Diagnostic and Statistical Manual of Mental Disorders. Second Edition*. Washington: APA

DSM-I. 1952. *Diagnostic and Statistical Manual of Mental Disorders. First Edition*. Washington: APA

Duma. 2002. "Minutes of the Meeting of the Lower House of the Parliament on 11.09.2002" [Стенограмма заседания Государственной думы, 11.09.2002 г., №148 (632)], Accessed 26.07.2018, http://pda.transcript.duma.gov.ru/node/1656/

Eco, Umberto. 1976. *A Theory of Semiotics*. Bloomington: Indiana UP

Esquirol, Etienne. 1845. *Mental Maladies: A Treatise on Insanity*. London: Lea and Blanchard

Felman, Shoshana. 2003. *The Scandal of the Speaking Body*. Stanford: Stanford UP

Fenichel, Otto. 2014. *The Psychoanalytic Theory of Neuroses*. New York & London: Routledge

Fenster, Marc. 1999. *Conspiracy Theories*. Minneapolis: Minnesota UP

Foucault, Michel. 1997. *Essential Works of Michel Foucault 1954–1984*. Vol. 3. *Power*. New York: New Press

Foucault, Michel. 1978. *The History of Sexuality*. Vol. 1. New York: Pantheon

58 *Desire*

Freud, Sigmund. 1962. "The Aetiology of Hysteria", *Standard Edition of the Complete Works of Sigmund Freud* 3: 189–224, London: Hogarth

Freud, Sigmund. 1958. "Psycho-analytic Notes on an Autobiographical Account of a Case of Paranoia", in *Standard Edition of the Complete Works of Sigmund Freud*. Vol. 12, 9–84, London: Hogarth.

Freud, Sigmund. 1951. "The Psychogenesis of a Case of Homosexuality in a Woman", *Standard Edition of the Complete Works of Sigmund Freud* 18: 145–72, London: Hogarth

Garfinkel, Harold. 1967. *Studies in Ethnomethodology*. Englewood Cliffs: Prentice Hall.

Global Research. 2018. "About Centre for Research on Globalization." Accessed 24.07.2018, www.globalresearch.ca/about-2

Glynos, Jason. 2001. "The Grip of Ideology: A Lacanian Approach to the Theory of Ideology", *Journal of Political Ideologies* 6, no. 2: 191–214

Glynos, Jason and David Howarth. 2007. *Logics of Critical Explanation in Social and Political Theory*. London: Routledge

Griesinger, Wilhelm. 1867. *Mental Pathology and Therapeutics*. London: New Sydenham Society

Hardt, Michael and Antonio Negri. 2001. *Empire*. Harvard: Harvard UP

Hofstadter, Richard. 1996. *The Paranoid Style in American Politics and Other Essays*. Cambridge, MA: Harvard UP

Horkheimer, Max and Theodor Adorno. 2002. *Dialectic of Enlightenment*. Stanford: Stanford UP

Knight, Peter. 2008. "Outrageous Conspiracy Theories: Popular and Official Responses to 9/11 in Germany and the United States", *New German Critique* 103: 165–93

Knight, Peter. 2000. *Conspiracy Culture: From Kennedy to the X Files*. London & New York: Routledge

Knight, Peter and Michael Butter. 2016. "Bridging the Great Divide: Conspiracy Theory Research for the 21st Century." *Diogenes*

Kraepelin, Emil. 2012. *Clinical Psychiatry*. London: Palgrave Macmillan

Lacan, Jacques. 2002. "The Subversion of the Subject and the Dialectic of Desire in the Freudian Unconscious", in *Écrits*, 671–702, New York & London: Norton

Lacan, Jacques. 1993. *The Seminar of Jacques Lacan: Book 3: The Psychoses 1956–1957*. New York & London: Norton

Lacan, Jacques. 1991. *The Seminar of Jacques Lacan: Book 17: The Other Side of Psychoanalysis 1969–1970*. New York & London: Norton

Lacan, Jacques. 1988. *The Seminar of Jacques Lacan: Book 2: The Ego in Freud's Theory and in the Technique of Psychoanalysis 1954–1955*. Cambridge: Cambridge UP

Lacan, Jacques. 1967. "Proposition on 9 October 1967 on the Psychoanalyst of the School." Accessed 20.07.2018, http://iclo-nls.org/wp-content/uploads/Pdf/Propositionof9October1967.pdf

Lacan, Jacques. 1963. "The Seminar of Jacques Lacan. Book X. Anxiety, 1962–1963." Accessed 20.07.2018, www.valas.fr/IMG/pdf/THE-SEMINAR-OF-JACQUES-LACAN-X_l_angoisse.pdf

Lacan, Jacques. 1959. "The Seminar of Jacques Lacan. Book VI. Desire and Its Interpretation, 1958–1959." Accessed 20.07.2018, www.lacaninireland.com/web/wp-content/uploads/2010/06/THE-SEMINAR-OF-JACQUES-LACAN-VI.pdf

Lacan, Jacques. 1958. "The Seminar of Jacques Lacan. Book V. The Formations of the Unconscious, 1957–1958." Accessed 20.07.2018, www.valas.fr/IMG/pdf/THE-SEMINAR-OF-JACQUES-LACAN-V_formations_de_l_in.pdf

Laclau, Ernesto. 2002. *The Populist Reason*. London: Verso

Laclau, Ernesto. 1996. *Emancipations*. London: Verso

Laclau, Ernesto. 1991. "The Impossibility of Society", *Canadian Journal of Political and Social Science* 15, no. 1/3: 24–7

Laclau, Ernesto and Chantal Mouffe. 1985. *Hegemony and Socialist Strategy: Towards a Radical Democratic Politics*. London: Verso

Lasègue, Charles and Jules Falret. 2008. "Shared Delusion", in *Anthology of French Language Psychiatric Texts*, edited by François-Régis Cousin, Jean Garrabé and Denis Morozov, 199–212, New York: John Wiley & Sons

Melley, Timothy. 2012. *The Covert Sphere: Secrecy, Fiction, and the National Security State*. Ithaca: Cornell UP

Miller, Iona. 2018. "Iona Miller Home." Accessed 16.07.2018, https://ionamiller.weebly.com/

Miller, Iona and Richard Miller. 2003. "Schumann Resonance and Human Psychobiology." Accessed 16.07.2018, http://biophysics.50megs.com/guest_book.html

Neumann, Franz. 1957. *The Democratic and the Authoritarian State*. Glencoe: Free Press

Nietzsche, Friedrich. 1998. *On the Genealogy of Morality*. Indianapolis: Hackett

O'Neill, Juliet. 1998. "Battling Mainstream Economy." *Ottawa Citizen*, 05.01.1998, Accessed 24.07.2018, https://web.archive.org/web/20031205084118/http://globalresearch.ca/articles/ONE311A.html

Popper, Karl. 1966. *The Open Society and Its Enemies*. London: Routledge

Popper, Karl. 1962. *Conjectures and Refutations: The Growth of Scientific Knowledge*. New York: Routledge

Scheler, Max. 2007. *Ressentiment*. Milwaukee: Marquette UP

Sérieux, Paul and Joseph Capgras. 2008. "The Reasoning Insanities. Delusion of Interpretation", in *Anthology of French Language Psychiatric Texts*, edited by François-Régis Cousin, Jean Garrabé and Denis Morozov, 447–58, New York: Wiley

Shorter, Edward. 2005. *A Historical Dictionary of Psychiatry*. Oxford: Oxford UP

Showalter, Elaine. 1997. *Hystories: Hysterical Epidemics and Modern Culture*. New York: Picador

Stavrakakis, Yannis. 2007. *The Lacanian Left: Psychoanalysis, Theory, Politics*. Edinburgh: Edinburgh UP

Stavrakakis, Yannis. 2002. *Lacan and the Political*. London: Routledge

Wacquant, Loïc. 2009. *Punishing the Poor*. Durham: Duke UP

Wacquant, Loïc. 1999. "Inside 'The Zone'", in *The Weight of the World: Social Suffering in Contemporary Society*, edited by Pierre Bourdieu, 140–67, Cambridge, MA: Polity

Žižek, Slavoj. 2018. *The Courage of Hopelessness: A Year of Acting Dangerously*. Brooklyn: Melville

Žižek, Slavoj. 2012. *Less Than Nothing*. London: Verso

Žižek, Slavoj. 2010. *Violence*. London: Profile

Žižek, Slavoj. 2007. *The Universal Exception*. London: Continuum

Žižek, Slavoj. 2001. *The Fragile Absolute: Or, why is the Christian Legacy Worth Fighting For?* London: Verso

Žižek, Slavoj. 1999. *The Ticklish Subject: The Absent Center of Political Ontology*. London: Verso

Žižek, Slavoj. 1997. "The Big Other Does Not Exist", *Journal of European Psychoanalysis* 5. Accessed 28.11.2016, www.psychomedia.it/jep/number5/zizek.htm

Žižek, Slavoj. 1992. *Enjoy Your Symptom!* New York: Routledge

3 Power and truth

The first two chapters focused on what makes conspiracy theorists claim impossible knowledge – suffering from the outside, desire from the inside. This chapter will try to explain how such knowledge claims are possible.
Knowledge has conditions of possibility that we usually take for granted. The problem of conspiracy knowledge is important because it is detached from many of those conditions. This chapter will analyze the condition of power.
Knowledge involves power for at least three reasons. Firstly, knowledge is generally legitimized by a reference to authority. Secondly, knowledge is essential to the operation of power because, without knowledge, any power would not be able to identify its objects or calculate its intervention. Thirdly, knowledge produces power effects, such as the knowledge of health risks making a person control her behavior more meticulously than any tyrant.
Knowledge detached from power is powerless. But conspiracy theories claim knowledge against power and nevertheless produce power effects significant enough to make them objects of research and concern, perhaps objects of concerned research.
How, then, is powerless knowledge possible? How does it produce power effects? And how it can have the value of truth?

Parrhesia

The mechanism of powerless knowledge can be described by the concept of parrhesia.
Parrhesia and the other Foucauldian concepts used in this chapter are historically situated constellations of forms of knowledge, relations of power, and modes of formation of the subject (Foucault 2008b, 9), but they are also diagrams that map out social forces and functions (Deleuze 1988, 34). I will try to distill their diagrammatic plane and use it as a background against which to describe the distinguishing features of conspiratorial claims to impossible knowledge.

In order to do that, let me substitute for the classical genealogy of par-rhesia an imaginary scene in which one publicly says to a tyrant that he is a tyrant (Foucault 2008a, 55).

Perhaps she is telling the truth. But she also claims knowledge against power that cannot be verified. Usually, we verify knowledge by games of true and false, but in this case, the game of true and false cannot be played simply by pointing out facts.

Facts are generally agreed upon by all; they make anybody respond with agreement. But let us assume that she points out an injustice, perhaps a banal violence covered by a conspiracy of silence. How could she expect an agreeable answer? The tyrant is not in her power, so he can always avoid her question, answer it ambiguously, or deny (Foucault 2008a, 88). And the tyrant is speaking before a public that supports him, or at least is used to him.

But if she cannot defeat the tyrant in a game of true and false, how can she claim any knowledge against him?

To explain that, we should take into account that accusing a tyrant of being a tyrant is not merely an act of frank speech. It means to claim that the tyrant does not have the right to exercise the power as he does, that he is not entitled to his power, and in that sense it means to claim his power. Parrhesia is nothing but a private revolution.

But then how is a private revolution possible?

Corruption

Can an act of parrhesia overflow into a conspiracy theory?

Since the question could sound weird in the context of weird conspiracy theories, let us take a more trivial example.

Corruption cannot be eradicated by government, but it cannot be tolerated, either.

Corruption cannot be eradicated because it is a transversal network of alliances between small groups which exchange gifts and counter-gifts, not so much above or against legality, but rather in the loopholes of the legal order (Deleuze 1988, 29). But corruption cannot be tolerated because its network is undermining the institutional authority, as if it is a primitive society inscribed in the modern state (Deleuze 1988, 35; Deleuze and Guattari 1987, 317–18).

Late modern governmentality tends to dissolve this double bind by developing apparatuses of security, set for endless fighting against corruption, apparatuses for policing the political that do not operate as a political police as far as they exercise their power in the mode of iusticium, i.e. as sovereign auctoritas, which restores the legitimacy of juridico-political order by suspending it in a state of exception (Agamben 2005, 50–1, 79).[1]

In line with this global governmental rationality, in the spring of 2011 the Indian government planned to establish an apparatus of security intended to fight corruption. But the anti-corruption activist Anna Hazare claimed that the government only pretended to fight corruption, that the government had stolen the independence of his country, and now the struggle for independence had to begin again (TNN 2011).

If Hazare was able to verify his claim, he would have brought a lawsuit against the government, as he had done before. Was he claiming impossible knowledge? Was he a conspiracy theorist?

Of course, the government dismissed Hazare's allegations, but this was a miscalculated response because he was not making a statement which would empower the government to agree or disagree; he was questioning its power in the name of truth. Responding to an act of parrhesia as if it was a question of true and false meant failing to respond to the questioning, taking one's power for granted, treating one's power as a fact that did not depend on right, and was not open for debate. Soon, the government would desperately try to repair its powerless response by violence.

Hazare decided to prove his claim by publicly fasting (BBC 2011). A couple of days later, he was joined by 150 others and supported by millions on social media and TV screens. Why was his act so successful, if he could not verify what he was talking about?

On the other hand, why was Hazare's act so singular? Two months later a popular guru, Ramdev, the head of a multimillion-dollar corporation, tried to repeat it with only limited success (PTI 2011a). Of course, Ramdev's public fast was stopped by the police. Yet, after two more months, the police tried to stop Hazare from starting another fast, but now they seemed powerless rather than overpowering, and the intervention provoked massive nation-wide protests (PTI 2011b).[2]

Feeling that the government was losing ground in a fight that should have been impossible, in the coming months supporters of the government claimed that Hazare's allegations were indeed a conspiracy theory and responded with other conspiracy theories, like an investigation into money illegally spent on his birthday (IndLaw 2011) or that his protests were covertly orchestrated by foreign governments (News18 2011). But this was again a miscalculated response because parrhesia was irreducible to the boldness or the arrogance of speaking frankly against the other, and its effects did not depend only on sincerity.

After four days of fasting, the government gave up. Did that mean that it recognized the truth of Hazare's claim? Thousands hailed the activist as he ended his fast to join the committee on anti-corruption legislation. The struggle had just begun, announced Hazare, and now he was telling a truth questioned by nobody (TNN 2011). Was that a victory?

Later, many would claim that his act was exploited by the opposition, by powerful non-governmental organizations like Rashtriya Swayamsevak Sangh (Das 2018), or that Hazare contributed to the ascendance of populism in India (Chatterjee 2012). But did that mean that he was not telling the truth when he denounced corruption?

No matter how one answers such difficult questions, they already show that the truth of parrhesiastic acts is not unquestionably guaranteed by their contents or by their effects. Then what is the dividing line between parrhesia and conspiracy theories?

In order to be able to address that question, we need to be equipped with a concept applicable to parrhesia not only as a general regime of veridiction or as a form of care for the self, as it is usually conceived, but also to individual speech acts.

Passionate speech

In order to explain the conditions of possibility of parrhesia, let us compare it with performatives.

Performatives are speech acts which do what they say in saying it, such as declaring a marriage, grading a paper, promising, and betting (Austin 1962, 6–7).

Like parrhesia, performative acts do not depend on games of true and false. Indeed, what sense it would make to verify a declaration of marriage? Since the value of performatives consists of what they do with words, they are rather successful or unsuccessful (Austin 1962, 16).

A performative act is successful if it is grounded on right: the subject of enunciation must have the right to say the words, they must be the right words, the words must be said in the right circumstances, the subject and the other participants in the act must have the right feelings and intentions, and they must commit themselves to the words and meet the commitment in their future behavior (Austin 1962, 15).

The right to perform a speech act depends on conventions (Austin 1962, 14). Such conventions are rarely written rules. More often they are regularities which – just like the norms of everyday life – become noticeable if they are breached. And even when the conventions are preestablished, their meaning in the particular circumstances is underdetermined and their application involves a practical accomplishment (Garfinkel 2002, 199–200; Coulter 1987, 39–40).

In order to illustrate such conventions, imagine that instead of addressing the tyrant, the parrhesiast decides to declare a revolution. It might seem that the revolutionary situation frees her from any convention. But what if she declares the revolution on behalf of unsuspecting others? What if she makes her daring declaration after a couple of beers, or at home in front of the TV screen? What if, instead of doing something revolutionary after that, she bursts into laughter? She will have violated the conventions that give her the right to speak like that, and in effect her performative act will be an instance of misfire or misuse. Her words will do nothing; she will have spoken nothing but words.

The dependence of performative acts on conventions is important because if we know the conventions of a performative act, we usually know what we are doing when we are performing it, and in that sense the act is predictable (Foucault 2008a, 62).

In contrast, parrhesia is not grounded on conventions (Foucault 2008a, 62).[3] Nevertheless, parrhesia involves right, because otherwise, it would be nothing more than an allegation, perhaps even a calumny. Therefore, the parrhesiast must establish her right by improvising with the existing conventions or by inventing new ones, so as to fulfill the following conditions:[4]

1   She should single out the other she is addressing.
2   She should declare herself entitled to address the other.
3   She should demand the response of the other in kind.
4   She should demand the response now. (Cavell 2006, 180–1)

Unlike conventions, improvisations are not publicly recognized, and the other can resist them by claiming that he is not the one that she should address, by claiming that she is not entitled to address him, by not responding in kind, or by avoiding or deferring his response (Cavell 2006, 181). Therefore, to establish her right, the parrhesiast should make the other recognize it, and in that sense she must win it in a fight against the other.[5]

However, parrhesia is not simply a fight with the other; it is not a quarrel, because quarrels tend to produce symmetrical rights, and you may have noticed that after a quarrel everyone usually feels righteous, at least for oneself. In contrast, parrhesiastic right is asymmetric, because if the parrhesiast is right, then the other is not.

The situation of the parrhesiast is even more complicated because the other is powerful, she is in his power, and she cannot appeal to a superior power that could enforce her asymmetric right, as in the case of legal rights against the state. Then, how is it possible for the powerless to make the powerful recognize her right?

It is possible because the parrhesiast takes a risk. In our imaginary example, she probably risks her life or at least her walk of life. But since the example might make parrhesia seem distant, we should also bear in mind other examples which suggest that the stake of the parrhesiastic act can be not only life or death but also risking one's standing among the others or one's relationship with the other, like risking one's popularity by speaking against the hegemonic opinion or risking the friendship of the other by telling her that she has done something deeply wrong (Foucault 2001b, 16). Risk is constitutive of the parrhesiastic act if the parrhesiast is free to avoid it. In that case, to take the risk of speaking against the powerful is an act of courage (Foucault 2008a, 66). But, in order to be successful, the parrhesiastic act must meet one more condition. If courage seems an accidental audacity, its meaning would consist of not what the parrhesiast is saying but what makes her talk like that, and so the act would dissolve in the tangled web of the causes of her suffering or in the endless chain of empty signifiers produced by her displaced desire. In order to be able to support the act, the courage of the parrhesiast should be rooted in the singular truth about herself, about her conduct toward herself and toward the others, and in that sense her courage should represent her ethos (Foucault 2008a, 158, 2008b, 25).

Now, if the parrhesiast has shown such courage and the tyrant punishes her, he will violate her ethos, and therefore he will display himself as unethical (Foucault 2008b, 12–13). In effect, he will demonstrate that she was right to denounce him as a tyrant. Indeed, is not that the power of the powerless, an ethos which makes the exercise of power over them seem an abuse of power?

Since parrhesia depends on the courage to take a risk, and risks are essentially unpredictable, then in contrast with performatives, parrhesiastic acts are successful as far as they are unpredictable, as far as the public, the other, and even the parrhesiast herself do not know what they are doing with their words or, more properly, what their words will do to them (Foucault 2008a, 62).

In sum, a parrhesiastic act is successful if the parrhesiast improvises with conventions in order to claim an unrecognized right against the other and justifies her claim by the test of a fight with the other, which requires courage, involves significant risks, and produces unpredictable outcomes. We can condense the conditions of possibility of parrhesia by representing it as a duel – a discursive duel against another, who has the power to wound.

But what if the parrhesiast is unable to meet one or more of the conditions of possibility of her act?

What if she fails to single out the other, or declare that she is entitled to address him, or establish courage as her ethos? What if the other does not respond, or does not respond in kind, or defers his response? What if the risk is not real? And what if the parrhesiast loses the duel with the other?

Then the parrhesiast will fail to establish her right, but her act will not disappear, as the infelicitous or insincere performatives do not disappear and still produce perlocutive effects (for example, one can still respond with laughter or tears to a misguided wedding ceremony or hold another responsible for a forfeited promise).

If the conditions of possibility of the parrhesiastic act are not met, it becomes an instance of bad, unsuccessful, infelicitous parrhesia, i.e. parrhesia that is lacking value as a forfeited coin. In the rest of this chapter, I argue that as far as conspiracy theories fail to establish the truth, we can describe them as infelicitous parrhesiastic acts.

The offstage

If conspiracy theories fail to meet the conditions of possibility of parrhesiastic acts, how are they able to produce effects?

In order to explain this, let us take another case of passionate denouncement of corruption. In February 2013, Bulgaria was shaken by mass protests against exorbitant energy prices. The government resigned, a coalition of the former opposition parties came to power, and a couple of weeks later the prime minister appointed a new director of the State Agency for National Security, Delyan Peevski, a man in his thirties. Peevski was a member of the parliament, an owner of television, newspaper, and online news outlets and a business empire, son of the former director of the national lottery, and until recently, a silent ally of the former government. A couple of hours after his appointment, the central square of the capital was crowded with protesters.

Respondent No. 14 was one of them, a woman in her forties, seemingly well-educated, working as a PR representative for a non-governmental organization.[6] She explained the reason for the sudden outburst of mass anger that brought her to the square:

> The offstage. Delyan Peevski is the emanation of the substitution of false for true, in which you do not have a real career. . . . This is not the American dream, if we can translate like that in Bulgarian the values with which we were nurtured, and we applauded and told to ourselves, well, if America is different from the Soviet Union. . . . Well, you must work, learn, excel in everything, you must prove yourself, and then the things in your life happen and are put in order. Even if I was educated in the communist period, I was nurtured like that. Those were the communist values. . . . [Peevski] is not one thing he claims to be, and for that reason he is an emanation of the offstage. . . . No, he is not demonized. He represents what he represents. And he cannot hide it anymore, because he was a very well kept secret, and it is because of the silence around him that his career happened like this.
>
> (Vajsova 2018, 166, 174)

What did 'the offstage' mean?

Respondent No. 14 explained that it was a network of exchange hidden from the public, an exchange of words, promises, favors, loyalties, gifts and counter-gifts, capital and power, transgression and immunity which was constitutive of the current political system, as if a primitive society based on personal affiliations had secretly captured the state apparatus.

Was that not a conspiracy theory?

According to Respondent No. 14, 'the offstage' was secret but also transparent, an open secret, "conspiracy in broad daylight" (Arendt 1972, 255–6, 36–41). Open secrets are not simply unknown; they are representations of content that is withheld from knowledge (Birchall 2015), like unknowns in mathematics, or like neurotic symptoms that actually point to a repressed desire. Since such open secrets are both kept and revealed, since their representation forecloses the truth about them, they escape the oppositions between true and false, intentional and unintentional, belief and disbelief, good faith and bad faith, and in effect they are unassimilable to the field of truthful discourse (Derrida 2005, 68–9).

As Respondent No. 14 conceived of 'the offstage' as an open secret, she could articulate it only as a counter-truth, as an empty symptom of truth withheld from knowledge. Perhaps if we needed a definition of conspiracy theories, we could define them as 'the offstage.' But how was such a definitive conspiracy theory able to bring a middle-aged, well-educated professional to the square?

As did most protesters, Respondent No. 14 answered that question by describing an act of passion which suddenly interrupted her everyday life (Vajsova 2018, 156). But, then, how could passion be something more than a cry or an outcry? How was it possible that passion became politically effective?

Later, the protesters would tell different stories and give different reasons for their passion, but at the square, their cumulative voice articulated only the passionate utterance 'Who?'

The government interpreted it as a question. The prime minister explained that it was he who nominated Peevski and that he would revoke the nomination.

But the protesters kept on asking by shouting in the streets day after day, by wearing badges with their empty question, by representing its affective value through artistic performances, witty slogans, beautiful photographs distributed in the news outlets and the social media, by giving ardent explanations before the TV cameras. Of course, 'Who?' overflowed into other passionate utterances like "Resignation!", and later to "Red garbage!", or to the much-debated phrase of one renown Bulgarian writer that the protesting man was clever and beautiful.

The insistent passion of the protesters turned their conspiratorial question into parrhesia, an act of speaking against the government the truth that it was powerless, that its power was controlled and exploited by offstage actors.

Was that parrhesiastic act felicitous?

The protesters successfully singled out the government and demonstrated their right to address it. But they demanded from the government an impossible response – who was pulling its strings offstage. And the government failed to respond. Instead of addressing the passionate utterance of the protest, the government tried to argue that the protesters were only a minority, a small social group of educated middle-class professionals who did not represent the population of the capital, let alone the country. Of course, there were the insinuations that someone was pulling their strings. The government failed to respond because it failed to realize that responding to a parrhesiastic act articulated as a conspiracy theory with another conspiracy theory is not a response in kind, but simply an altercation.

More importantly, the conditions of possibility of the parrhesiastic act were eroded by the fact that the government soon retreated into silence. In consequence, the protesters were no longer exposed to risk, their protest came to be increasingly detached from the ethos of courage, and in a couple of months the passionate masses melted down to an angry group of anti-communists who roamed the streets every other evening shouting "Resignation!" and "Red garbage!"

In the final analysis, the parrhesiastic act of the protesters was unsuccessful; it ended in noise and disappointment, and it brought back to power the former governing party, which increasingly started to seem to be the only game in town. The passionate utterance 'Who?' was initially an attempt at parrhesia, but it started to seem nothing but a conspiracy theory.[7]

Nevertheless, the act was effective because its infelicity demonstrated the inability of the government to respond and therefore the irresponsibility of the government. It was a duel rather than communication, and a conspiracy theory wrapped in an act of bad parrhesia turned out to be a powerful weapon.

Subjugated knowledge

Detached from knowledge, parrhesia would be nothing but a scream. But how can it be grounded on knowledge if it is not a game of true and false?

In order to understand that, we need a concept of knowledge that does not reduce it to verifiable propositions. At the same time, the concept will be inadequate if it is unable to explain how we make such propositions.

Let us assume that knowledge is a field formed by a discursive practice (Foucault 1989, 201).

Of course, that does not mean that knowledge is limited to the sayable. Imagine for example that one does not feel well, and she wants to know what is causing this feeling. So she tries to define it, perhaps only tentatively, as we usually define our everyday problems, and she says to herself that she is feeling depressed. This will probably leave no discernible trace and she will not even write it down, but it is still a discursive event.

What is the significance of that discursive event?

Let us assume that the signified of 'depression' is a dysphoric mood (DSM-III 1980, 210). But knowing the signified is hardly enough. The significance of her statement is something else, something more, and in order to know what it is, instead of ascending to the level of thought or descending to the material fluidity of affect, she will probably try to find out more.

Imagine that she is searching information on the internet and retrieves a series of statements, for example that depression is a common and serious medical illness which affects how you feel, think, and act. If she is right to say that she is feeling depressed, if she knows what she is talking about, then her statement can be inscribed in that series as another statement about depression, as a variation of the series of statements about depression (Foucault 1989, 41;Deleuze 1988, 5–6).

But such series of statements are not random; they are formed by regularities that map out how one can speak about depression (Foucault 1989, 82, 201). For example, some statements warn her about dangers, others advise her to see a doctor, yet others are composed as personal narratives or as popular explanations of the biochemical mechanism of depression. And their diverging lines of variation delineate a concept of depression which for our purposes can be reduced to symptomatology and conceived of as a sort of discursive relay assembled from conditional statements of the type 'if . . . then. . . . ' For example, if her mood disturbance is prominent and persistent, and she has poor appetite, insomnia, fatigue, and a feeling of worthlessness for more than two weeks, then she can describe her situation by the concept of a major depressive episode (DSM-III 1980, 213).

Then what is the significance of loss of appetite or insomnia?

They are variables, the actual value of which depends on her feeding or sleeping patterns, which belong to the plane of the visible. Although she understands the meaning of insomnia or loss of appetite, they would be nothing but words and would lack any real significance if she does not cross from the plane of the sayable to the plane of the visible by articulating them as objects. But if she does that, if she objectifies her situation as depression, then she articulates herself as a depressive subject. In effect, her attempt to know 'what it is' will put her in her place in the social order as an individual suffering from affective disorder or as a member of the population affected by the depression epidemic (Foucault 1989, 49–50; Deleuze 1988, 39).

Furthermore, her self-diagnosis opens up a horizon of potential events associated with risks such as thoughts of suicide, deterioration to psychosis, or remission. The statement about her depression therefore opens up a field of intervention. Let us say that she consults a doctor, who recommends the appropriate medication and fills in the appropriate documents. Then her statement has triggered medical, economic, and administrative apparatuses that can bring into action other apparatuses (Deleuze 1988, 9). The intervention of such apparatuses of power will exert a powerful retroactive effect on her because it will constitute her as a responsible and rational subject, able to control the risks of her suffering before they turn into a ruinous force (Rose 1999, xxiii).

Through being constituted as a rational subject inscribed in an objective place in the social order, she will know 'what it is' with her. But to come to knowledge, she made a statement, gave it a regular form, inscribed it in a series of other statements, associated it with a concept, defined its objects, developed a mode of approaching those objects, positioned herself as a subject, and initiated the intervention of apparatuses of power (Foucault 1989, 201). It is in that sense that knowledge is a field formed by discursive practice – it is grounded on a work of ordering that holds together the visible and the sayable by the exercise of some power (Deleuze 1988, 39;Badiou 2005, 328–9).

However, this is valid for many forms of knowledge that we would hesitate to call science, including searching for information on the internet. Scientific knowledge is distinguished from such popular knowledge by its powerful order (Deleuze 1988, 19).

To be organized as a science, knowledge has to be differentiated as an autonomous field with its own game of true and false and its own pragmatic conventions, and in that sense it has to cross the thresholds of positivity, epistemologization, and scientificity (Foucault 1989, 205–6,1981, 60).

But crossing these thresholds is a product of historically situated work that involves at least the following operations (Foucault 2004, 180):

1 The selection of knowledges of general value; hence the elimination or disqualification of knowledges that are too petty, local, or limited, because of which their generalization would be costly and ineffective

2 Normalization, adaptation, and harmonization of the dispersed knowledges aimed to make them comparable with each other, measurable against each other, and translatable into each other, so that they can be exchanged and circulate effectively

3 Hierarchical classification aimed at founding the more practical or particular knowledges on knowledge that is more fundamental or abstract, so as to allow the control of the lower levels of the hierarchy by means of higher-order knowledge

4   Pyramidal centralization of the order of knowledges, which stimulates the communication between the different hierarchical levels, and at the same time stabilizes the asymmetrical distribution of the power to know through its institutionalization

But the same work of ordering forms the grid of any disciplinary power. Therefore, scientific knowledge is disciplined knowledge; it is knowledge ordered into disciplines, and because of that it is also disciplinary knowledge, policing of knowledges (Foucault 2004, 187, 1981, 61).[8]

Of course, disciplinary knowledge rose to hegemony not because of some insidious violence but rather because it brought important advantages:

1   Premodern knowledge was artisanal, and since it was learned as an art by a long process of training in theory and practice, it could not be detached from its subject. In contrast, the truth-value of disciplinary knowledge does not depend on its subject, just like the correctness of a formula does not depend on who is writing it (Foucault 1981, 59, 2009, 24).

2   Since premodern knowledge required a long and incalculable training, it was costly. Disciplinary knowledge can be accumulated, communicated, and acquired at a significantly lower cost. In effect, it can circulate faster and it allows more intensive development and progressively growing performativity (Foucault 2004, 184, 1981, 63; Lyotard 1984, 46–7).

3   Knowledge is essentially open to questioning, and it casts a shadow of counter-knowledge. The premodern order of knowledge tried to repel counter-knowledge as unorthodoxy. In contrast, scientific disciplines control not the contents of knowledge claims but the right to claim knowledge, by means of an asymmetrical distribution of the right to speak in the name of science, guaranteed through institutional apparatuses like the university, the publishing industry, or copyright. Because of that, science is able to integrate counter-knowledge, to analyze its nature, to reconcile it with other knowledges, and to harness its productivity (Foucault 2004, 184, 1981, 63).

But if scientific knowledge is grounded on disciplinary order, it is also knowledge about order. And since to know means to be able to make verifiable statements, then in the case of science it also means to know how to put the statements in order. In that sense, scientific statements are perhaps the purest form of order-words (Deleuze and Guattari 1987, 77–81).

The concept of legitimacy of knowledge is intended to capture precisely this self-referential knowledge about order, superimposed over the knowledge of particular objects. To know legitimately means to know what the true order of knowledge is, how to order the statements so as to guarantee their truth-value, and what can be ordered by means of true statements. In that sense, legitimation of knowledge is a second-order game of true and false.[9]

What if some knowledge is disqualified by this second-order game as illegitimate?

Illegitimate knowledge is not necessarily ignorance. Take for example local knowledge, like what it costs to work somewhere, or singular knowledge, like how the things work out with this particular manager. Other examples are knowledge about the infinitesimal differences in our everyday routines that make a difference only if they are accumulated, knowledge about the thresholds above which a discomfort becomes a problem, knowledge about latent variables that can change the whole situation, and the almost silent memory of conflicts that were perhaps too petty, trivial, or inconsequential to become history. Such knowledge is not ignorance, but it is too singular to be normalized, too costly to be exchanged with others, and too inefficient to justify any investment.

Therefore, such illegitimate knowledge is irredeemably marked by disorder. It is knowledge about the disorder characteristic of any act in our everyday lives, constitutive of any act that is not an automated activity. To inscribe such knowledge in the disciplinary order of science would be lack of knowledge, and it can produce nothing but a teratology (Foucault 1981, 60).

Following Michel Foucault, I will call such knowledges subjugated or rebellious:[10]

> When I say "subjugated knowledges," I mean two things. On the one hand, I am referring to historical contents that have been buried or masked in functional coherences or formal systematizations. . . . I am also referring to a whole series of knowledges that have been disqualified as nonconceptual knowledges, as insufficiently elaborated knowledges: naive knowledges, hierarchically inferior knowledges, knowledges that are below the required level of erudition and scientificity.
>
> (Foucault 2004, 7)

In the rest of this chapter I will assume that an act of parrhesia is a claim of right, and not merely a groan of suffering, because it is grounded on subjugated knowledge. But then, since conspiracy theories are infelicitous parrhesiastic acts, do they also involve subjugated knowledge?

Even the infelicitous parrhesiasts are certainly not like the teacher, who avoids the risk to her relationship with the others and justifies her knowledge by grafting it onto the mighty tree of those after whom she speaks (Foucault 1997, 24–5).[11]

Conspiratorial knowledge

Conspiracy theories that do not incorporate subjugated knowledge do not constitute acts; they are nothing but words.

On the other hand, parrhesiastic subjects who are infelicitously passing into act often give to their subjugated knowledge a form that can be seen as a conspiracy theory. Let me illustrate that by a claim of right widely perceived as conspiratorial.

In the winter of 2010, the Bulgarian government introduced regulations on genetically modified organisms (GMOs).

The general public interpreted the regulations as surreptitious deregulation because they contained loopholes that could be exploited by global corporations, and the sanctions for their violation were so minimalist that infringements seemed lucrative.

A loose coalition of ecological organizations and concerned mothers organized protests, which were initially neglected by the government and the media. But the protesters managed to articulate their demands as equivalent to the demands of heterogeneous social actors, including the national associations of consumers, beekeepers, grain producers, ecological farmers, and non-ecological farmers, as well as the national guild of chefs and a yoga club. The chain of equivalence was represented by the empty signifier of mothers concerned for the lives of their children.

In response, the government proposed to amend the regulations by further regulations and insinuated that since the protests could not be justified by scientific knowledge, they were driven by hidden motives, perhaps by a desire to bring down the government.[12] This conspiratorial theory of the protests was implicitly endorsed by experts who argued from the TV screen that the ban on GMOs demanded by the protesters would jeopardize the traditional Bulgarian people, that GMOs were actually healthier than the normal crops, that GMOs were actually safer because they were constantly tested in high-tech corporate laboratories, that GMOs could help allergies, and that GMOs were ultimately very useful to the bees.[13]

However, one of the protests against GMOs coincided with a mass protest against increased energy prices, and the mothers who spoke for the protesters finally got the attention of the media. But what could a mother say, apart from being concerned for her children? And if a mother tried to speak beyond her social position, how could she justify her claim against the experts?

Before the cameras, the nervous and excited mothers tried to explain why they were against GMOs. As the media attention was limited by the rhythm of the daily news, their arguments were distilled to the following:

> Protester 1: Our life depends on that, there is nothing more important than that. Protester 2: Because it is important that nature stays what it is for our children, and the food is as we know it. Protester 3: I hope that they will vote with common sense what the society wants, and not some ambiguous texts.
>
> (BNT 2010)

The statements lacked content. Yet they were articulated by work on the visible and the sayable, which allowed the mothers to discern a problem and to group the social actors by their positions on the issue: the legal order was changing, the changes involved risks that could not be reliably calculated, the price of the risks was too enormous to be covered by insurance, the government was trying to regulate the risks so as to redistribute them over the population; in consequence, their price would be paid by us, we did not want to pay for them, and we should not be made to pay for them, if we were free to govern our lives. And this was perhaps only the tip of an iceberg of discernment, classification, problematization, and possible lines of reasoning.

But the statements could not be purged of anxiety, they could not be abstracted from their subjects or from the situation, and they could not be normalized, harmonized, hierarchized, centralized, or disciplined, so they could not acquire a general value, let alone pass the thresholds of positivity, epistemologization, or scientificity. Because of that, the statements were grounded on subjugated knowledge, and they could be easily read as a conspiracy theory of GMOs. But did that mean that the protesters did not know what they were talking about?

I went to that protest.

Polemology of order

I have assumed that acts of parrhesia depend on subjugated knowledge.

But parrhesiastic knowledge is not the practical knowledge of the artisan, the private knowledge of the sufferer, or the tacit knowledge of everyday life because it has a normative dimension. The parrhesiast says not merely what she knows, but what must be known, even what must be known by another that does not want to know, because her knowledge is aimed at him as a weapon.

Parrhesiastic knowledge is not simply subjugated; it is rebellious knowledge. But how is it possible to use parrhesiastic knowledge effectively in a duel against a powerful other if it cannot be integrated into the general order of knowledge and can be easily disqualified by any game of true and false? The knowledge claimed by the parrhesiast can be defended by means of disqualifying the order of knowledge and its verification games. We can derive the rationale of such a defensive strategy from the discourse of race wars, which Foucault analyzed in the context of the disciplinarization of historical knowledge, if we try to discern through its historical contents a diagram of claims against the social order.

In order to understand the stake of the analysis, imagine that one wants to speak out against injustice. In such cases, we usually describe violations of the order, for example some infringement on a fundamental right such as equal treatment and respect. But what if one wants to speak out against injustice that is constitutive of the order, for example against social inequalities, which justification as outcomes of free competition is constitutive of capitalism? Would one not be claiming that it is unjust to lose a competition, that justice would require that nobody is a loser, and therefore there should be no competition? Or this is just an invitation for a revolution?

The discourse of race war was formed at the turn of the 16th century in a similar situation, in which different social actors made claims not against a particular injustice but rather against the injustice of the order itself, and they tried to justify their claims by subjugated knowledge about power, order, or history. The discursive practice can be outlined as follows (Foucault 2004, 53–138):

1   The society is split between oppressors and oppressed; the oppressors are a powerful minority, while the oppressed are a powerless majority (Foucault 2004, 88).
2   Since the oppressors and the oppressed have nothing in common, since they do not inhabit the same social world, they are represented as races – of course, not in the modern biological sense of race, but rather in the relational sense developed in early modernity, i.e. as a population marked off by its origin, religion, or social or economic status, which does not coincide with the population of the state (Foucault 2004, 65, 77).
3   The discourse of race war is structured so as to articulate the claim that the oppressed are entitled to what the powerful minority has taken from them, for example political emancipation, recognition of their origin or religion, an equal economic or social status, etc. Therefore, the power of the dominant minority is represented as violence (Foucault 2004, 110).
4   As the power of the dominant minority is rooted in the established social order, those who claim to speak on behalf of the oppressed challenge the order as an instrument of oppression, the tyrannical nature of which is disguised as legality, although it is only an ascendancy in

the unfinished war between the oppressors and the oppressed (Foucault 2004, 88).

5   The constitution of oppression as an order is explained by narratives about an originary violence that brought forth the current social order, such as a conquest, a war, a coup, or a clandestine stealing of power, as well as by quasi-mythic narratives about the peace and prosperity enjoyed by the majority before that act of originary violence (Foucault 2004, 98).

6   The originary violence that produced the social order could be justified as a response to other acts of violence, perhaps as a retribution or rectification, or by the need to maintain peace, or by the fact that the oppressed have chosen to accept their situation rather than to try and change it. The discourse of race war tries to foreclose such justifications by narratives about the secret resistance of the oppressed which contradict the history of the oppressors and therefore function as counterhistory (Foucault 2004, 70–3).

7   Since resistance against the oppressors is also resistance against the established order, it can be denounced as a crime or as a threat to security which is forestalled by speaking out against the injustice or impotence of the current order.

8   As far as the secret resistance against the established order does not make a difference, its ineffectiveness is justified by the need to enlighten the majority or by imaginary scenarios of the victory to come, which will end the oppression and restore harmony.

Foucault analyzed the discourse of race war on the basis of early modern examples like the myths about the Norman oppression of Anglo-Saxons or French narratives about the secretly oppressive nature of the ancien régime, which escalated into the Fronde.

However, Foucault claimed that modern biological state racism, the revolutionary discourse, and the discourse of class struggle are transformations of the discourse of race war (Foucault 2004, 60, 79–82, 134–8). Of course, he never addressed conspiracy theories, but I think that they can be described as another transformation of the concept of oppression, which emerged in the early modern discourse of race war.

Strategy of seduction

Although subjugated knowledge is excluded from the disciplinary order of modern science, it is not simply a knowledge disorder. It can be ordered differently, and in order to make it more defensible, conspiracy theories often organize it around a claim against oppression, the rationality of which is comparable to the discourse of race wars. Let me illustrate that by an affirmative conspiracy theory of biotechnology.

In 2003, 300 members of the Raelian movement, who had gathered for a conference on sensual meditation in Brazil, wrote with their naked bodies 'yes to GMO' (Agbiotech 2003). The performance was intended as a strong response to 30 British activists who wrote 'no to GMO' with their fully dressed bodies. But the naked bodies did not speak for themselves; they repeated a recent statement by Rael, the founder of their atheist religion, a visionary, sports journalist, and son of an alien.

Rael is also Claude Vorilhon, and if 'yes to biotechnology' would have been said by Vorilhon, it would be nothing more than a personal opinion. A scientist would have to say much more in order to sound scientific, as in fact did Rael's close associate Dr. Bosselier in announcing the first successful human cloning, which for a short while turned the movement into global news.

How was it possible to claim that a 'yes' to biotechnology had the value of truth?

Rael did not speak as a layman or a scientist but as a prophet. Of course, prophets are not parrhesiasts because they speak in the name of God rather than in their own name (Foucault 2008b, 15), but Rael is an atheist prophet, and he speaks in the name of the aliens who created life on Earth by advanced biotechnology 25,000 years ago.

In the times of the prophets, prophetic veridiction was not guaranteed by institutions, and its felicity depended on the future and on its positioning in a dynamic field of forces (Agamben 2005, 60–1). But to say 'yes' to biotechnology meant to affirm what was widely considered the future of science, so the future prophesized by Rael seemed scientifically guaranteed. In fact, the naked statement of his followers was ironically approved by Monsanto (Agbiotech 2003).

Since the 1970s, Rael has tried to position himself in the field of forces by criticizing religion in favor of spirituality, bourgeois family in favor of sexual emancipation, popular democracy in favor of geniocracy, disciplinary science in favor of research. The common denominator of such divergent positions was opposition to the institutions which produced the social reality that he wanted to transcend (Boltanski 2014, 15). To position himself as a prophet, Rael needed to undermine their power, and since he had at his disposal only the power of speech, he relentlessly attacked them with parrhesiastic acts, like the claim that the church exploited the guilt which it instilled in believers (Rael 2005a, 82).

However, Rael's parrhesiastic acts were doomed to infelicity since he was addressing virtual others, such as democracy in general rather than the government. Since the virtual others could respond only by silence, he tried to make their silence the object of his parrhesia and to denounce it as impotence.

But, in order to claim what was the meaning of silence, Rael needed to refer to knowledge, and since no particular knowledge could work, he referred to popular knowledge of the impotence of power derived from conspiracy theory about the social order: the political, religious, and academic elites keep their power by deresponsibilizing the people; although the aliens made each individual perfectly responsible for all her actions and forbade inflicting pain on others, the elites manipulate us by dissolving individual responsibility into fictions like the nation, the family, the law, or great causes; in effect, the elites free the people from responsibility in exchange for their obedience, and they wage war against anyone who wants to reclaim the responsibility for and the joy of his life (Rael 2005a, 316–17).

It would be a misunderstanding to read such conspiracy theories as attempts to provide a cognitive mapping alternative to the established social order because they depend on seduction rather than on cognition.[14] Let me explain that by summarizing the concept of seduction developed by Jean Baudrillard (1990):[15]

1   Seduction is grounded on representation.
2   Yet seduction cannot be represented. In fact, 'I seduce you' is no less inconceivable as a speech act than 'I offend you' (Austin 1962, 30).
3   Therefore, seduction is constituted as an open secret, the truth of which is foreclosed in the exchange with the other.
4   At the same time, seduction is articulated by this exchange, the constitutive rule of which is to respond to the other now and in kind.
5   Since what counts as a response in kind is not defined by preestablished conventions, the exchange is grounded on immanent and arbitrary rules, and in that sense it is structured as a game.
6   In contrast with passionate utterances, the result of a game of seduction depends on showing vulnerability rather than on attacking the vulnerabilities of the other. Therefore, as far as the stake of seduction is conquest or victory, it is a duel of weakness.
7   Since both actors respond to the other in kind, each one is mirroring the weakness of the other. Therefore, the signs of weakness produced by each one reflect the other. In that sense, seduction is a play of surfaces, and if it stirs desire, it is not repressed desire, the latent content of which is hidden in the depth of the subject; it is a superficial desire represented in the manifest content of the exchange between the actors as the open secret of their game.

How does the Raelian conspiratorial parrhesia seduce?

Let us take sexuality. According to Rael, the social order established by the church tried to repress sexuality and limit it to procreation. But the alien creators designed all our organs in all their functions, and using the organs for our pleasure should bring us happiness rather than shame (Rael 2005a, 186–7). The creators gave us no other rules on sexuality but to behave as we desire, as long as the others agree. Therefore, the church imposed artificial rules which already serve no purpose but to maintain its power by the insidious mechanism of sin. For example, the church decries prostitution, but it tolerates selling one's brain "to the weapons industry, which will use his knowledge to kill millions of people" (Rael 2005b). Prostitution will be indeed wrong when humanity starts living like the aliens who denounce anything except pleasure, but for now "we must leave everybody to live their life the way they want" (Rael 2005b).

Rael's conspiracy theory about the church would be a meaningless banality if it was not associated with parrhesiastic criticisms like the one of the military industry. But even though it was addressed to virtual others, it was performed before listeners who recognized in it their own double weakness before pleasure and guilt and who filled in the empty interpellation with a command to enjoy themselves with the phantasmatic scenarios of their own desires. Rael seemed to know what he was talking about not because he was conveying the message of the aliens but because his weakness before pleasure and guilt reflected theirs, because he was a mirror subject of pleasure and guilt, albeit one able to overcome the latter by awakening his mind through sensual meditation.

This game of seduction was powerful enough to attract a substantial number of followers working in the sex industry, who formed a group affiliated with the movement, Rael's Girls. Let me illustrate its effects by a testimony of a member of the group:[16]

> I was born and raised as a Muslim in France. . . . As a child and a teenager I was taught that sex was a taboo. . . . When I discovered the Raelian Philosophy, Sensual Meditation, (awakening the mind by awakening the body) . . . Whoaaaaaaaa!!! I could see how much I had to let go . . . I started asking myself questions about my own sexuality, and I realized how unconscious my thinking was from believing what my mom had always taught me. . . . Fantastic, around this time, I had my first orgasm, discovering more and more my body, myself, all the pleasure coming from it. . . . In fact, here I am today, I have been in the Raelian Movement for about 10 years and I am working as a Stripper, a job I have had for the last 4 years.
>
> (Raelgirls 2018)

The seductive weakness of Rael's conspiratorial parrhesia seemed so powerful that it became a concern for the United States embassy in Canada. Raelians were framed as a potential security risk as it seemed that they were planning to move to Florida, and their announcement of successful human cloning could lead to stricter Canadian regulations on biotechnology that would be unfavorable to United States interests (Kantor 2003; Cellucci 2002). In order to evaluate the risk, an operative even took care to collect information on Rael's real birth from a specialist, on his real goals from a local news analysts, and on the real number of his followers from an expert in new religious movements (Kantor 2003).

Later, the cables were included in the archive published by Wikileaks, and Julian Assange himself referred to them once or twice, hoping to seduce a wider audience by inscribing in the manifest content of his parrhesiastic act the innuendo that the governmental secrets he disclosed contained some information about aliens (Salla 2011).

But if the government was investigating the security risks posed by the Raelians, was it not engaged in a fight against threats barely discernible in the mutter of marginal minorities, a fight that was virtually endless? What if the government had become conspiratorial (Agamben, 2000, 126–8)? Was this not one of the most disturbing questions posed by the Wikileaks disclosures?

Techniques of the self

Parrhesiastic acts have a condition of possibility beyond passion, courage, and knowledge, and their power, even the seductive power of conspiratorial acts of bad parrhesia, depends also on that further condition. In order to explain it, let me compare once again parrhesiastic and performative acts.

Performative acts are explicit if they state what they do; for example, 'I promise' or 'I warn you.' But performatives can be also implicit. Imagine that someone is saying 'Bull!' Although she does not state her act, this is still a performative act because she is doing something with her words – she is warning you – and such an implicit performative can be rewritten in an explicit form without sounding odd (compare, for example, 'I warn you about the bull' and 'I declare that there is a bull'; Austin 1962, 32–3).

Parrhesiastic acts have implicit content because the parrhesiast does not just say the truth about the other; she also commits herself to the truth of what she says and to the act of saying it. If we take into account that implicit content, any act of parrhesia can be rewritten in the following explicit form:

> I tell the truth, and I truly think that it is true, and I truly think that I am saying the truth when I say it. . . . I am the person who has spoken this

truth; I therefore bind myself to the act of stating it, and take on the risk of all its consequences.

(Foucault 2008a, 64–5)

But then parrhesia involves at least three subjects: the speaking subject, the subject of the act, and the subject of the truth. If the parrhesiastic act is successful, those subjects should be identical, and if they are not, it will turn into bad parrhesia (Foucault 2008a, 64–5, 2001b, 13).

The coincidence of the subjects of the speech, truth, and act is not granted. Take for example the case of flattery, where the subject of the speech is split from the subject of the truth (Foucault 2001a, 373–5), or the case of anger, where the subjects of the speech and act are split from the subject of the truth (Foucault 2001a, 374). Or take for example everyday speech, where in speaking the truth we rarely meditate or commit ourselves to the act of its enunciation, and because of that, the proliferation of subjects characteristic of parrhesia seems redundant. Indeed, any common-sense phrase like 'I am depressed' would sound rather odd if it was rewritten as an explicit act of parrhesia: 'I truly think that I am saying the truth when I say that I am depressed, and I am the one who has spoken the truth about my depression; I therefore commit myself to the act of stating it, and take on the risk of all its consequences.'

Since the subjects involved in parrhesia are not necessarily identical, they must be identified. Therefore, the felicity of any parrhesiastic act depends on work, which transforms the everyday subject of speech, the self of everyday speech, into a subject of truth and commitment. And it is precisely in this sense that parrhesia is a pact of the parrhesiast with herself (Foucault 2008a, 64).

But, contrary to the hopes of contemporary popular psychology, the self is the result of a complex interplay of internal and external forces, and because of that, it cannot simply transform itself from the inside by the power of pure consciousness. The parrhesiastic transformation of the self, in particular, involves knowledge about the others and the social world, reflection on truths threateningly unrecognizable by the others, and commitment to lines of action that deviate from ordinary life, and it does not let the act of speaking the truth pass by like ordinary speech (Foucault 2008b, 9). Because of that, its principal effect is not that it makes the parrhesiast see herself differently; rather, it emancipates her from the others and enables her to govern herself (Foucault 2001a, 379, 385).

Since parrhesia transforms its subject, it is closely associated with techniques of the self, analyzed by Michel Foucault in the context of antiquity (Foucault 2017, 33). Indeed, the parrhesiastic speech of the master who risks his bond with the disciple in order to teach him to govern himself is the core of the care of the self (Foucault 2001a, 3667) and of the classical techniques of the self in general (Foucault 2008b, 4–5).

But if the transformations of techniques of the self can be traced to Christianity (Foucault 2008b, 5), or even to late modernity (Foucault 2008b, 29–30), are such techniques relevant to conspiracy theories? Perhaps conspiracy theories require knowledge, but do they involve reflection on the truth or committed work on oneself, and do they emancipate their subjects? And in what sense do they involve another? Because conspiracy theories, at least as they are usually pictured, seem consolations of solitude.

Self-transformation

Even though conspiracy theories are unsuccessful acts of parrhesia, they can produce powerful effects if they trigger a transformation of the self. Let me illustrate that by a case of personal transformation which passed through the point of doubt about medical conspiracy.

E. is suffering.[17] In the office, she is trying to invent different paths to the bathroom, hoping that the others will notice her trips less. The doctors diagnose her condition as irritable bowel syndrome and explain with the cause to be stress. She then takes part in a reality show about surviving in the wilderness, which makes a spectacle of starvation and she feels much better. So, she decides to diagnose herself.

After a period of reading and searching for information on the internet, after testing a number of foods that could be allergenic, she comes to the conclusion that she has celiac disease. But the doctors do not endorse her self-diagnosis. Why?

The inefficiency of diagnostics seems too general to be explained by the personalities of the doctors; it indicates the impotence of clinical medicine.[18] Is it ignorance or conspiracy? E. asks herself. Or is it perhaps ignorance caused by conspiracy?

E. does not answer that question; she only speculates that it is probably because gluten intolerance cannot be profitably treated. But another influential book on gluten intolerance will develop similar speculations into an argument: the profit margin of food can be increased if one sells not simply nutrition but desire, and the food industry managed to do that with advertisements, marketing techniques, and biochemical intensification of taste; since industrial food involves health risks, the food industry has ensured the support of relevant research institutions and professional organizations that vouch for its products and gloss over the risks. Because of this alliance between science and capitalism, gluten-based products have been widely promoted as healthy and have become an essential part of daily meals, although they are detrimental to many and even those who do not suffer from celiac disease or gluten intolerance could optimize themselves by avoiding them. In the last decades, the problem has become even graver because of genetically modified crops which contain far more gluten than the older varieties, and their detrimental effects are essentially concealed by mainstream research under the influence of the food industry (Davis 2011, 13, 33, 167–9).

The self-diagnosis makes E. transform her life and become a healthier and happier self, but the transformation comes at a price. Firstly, she is paying the price of daily asceticism. Since gluten is an ingredient of almost all products of the food industry, from pasta and bread to soy sauce, in fact even to the nutrition bars E. subsisted on while she was treated by a holistic healer, she needs to control every aspect of her diet.

Secondly, the asceticism transforms her relationships with others. Food is involved in many social activities, from coffee breaks at the office to eating out on a date, and E. is refusing food that is sanctioned as normal. For example, since E. was a child, her family has gathered on Sundays around the loaf of bread baked by her grandmother, and now she rejects it. Does that mean that she is rejecting the family? E. tries to explain that she cannot, but her condition has not been confirmed by a doctor, and it seems that she does not want to, without being able to explain why. 'Since when?' her loving grandmother keeps asking, until she finally starts making two loaves of bread on Sundays, one gluten-free especially for E.

Thirdly, the asceticism transforms her social world because it makes her read differently even the supermarket aisles, which start to seem a duel of seduction. The order of the products on the aisles is shaped by marketing strategies which try to exploit the weakness of the customers, for example by putting high-profit foods filled with gluten and sugar just in front of the cash registers, temporarily arresting customers' movement.[19] Or this is just another conspiracy theory?

However, E. learns how to resist the seductions of consumer capitalism, and when she reflects on herself, she finds that the asceticism helped her regain control over her body and her life and that she could not imagine returning to gluten, even if she was miraculously cured of her celiac disease. The truth is that she became a better, healthier, and stronger self, as well as a bestselling author of a book on the gluten-free lifestyle.

But is that enough to guarantee the truth of her transformation, to demonstrate that she is truly transformed, or to prove that it is the asceticism that has truly transformed her? She is not always this better and stronger self. At least while she is still in the process of transforming herself, on some days she doubts her self-diagnosis and even tries to eat gluten as a test. Indeed, what if her condition was never confirmed? Would she be any different from the conspiratorial minds who distrust clinical medicine and claim to discern behind the reassuring smile of the doctor the seductive machinery of biocapitalism (Rose 2007, 6–8)?

And the problem of truth in the case of E. is even further complicated by the reception of her book and by her later media career. What if her truth was shaped by another, subtler regime of power which has channeled her critique of the impotence of clinical medicine?

Foucault did not pursue his analysis of techniques of the self beyond the threshold of modernity, but the governmentality studies adapted his concept into an account of the new pastorate of the experts on living – therapists, counselors, healers, gurus, nutritionists, productivity coaches, and life coaches (Rose 2007, 73–5). Unlike Christian pastors, such experts on living promise salvation from the burden of one's current condition rather than from sin; they refer to contemporary medicine, biochemistry, genomics, anthropology, psychology, and management rather than to a doctrine; they command auton-omous choice and personal responsibility rather than obedience to spiritual direction; they enfold the knowledge they give or claim to give in practices of self-transformation intended to lead one to the truth of a better life, the truth that would make the life better (Rose 2007, 28, 73–5).

Yet the experts of living still compete on the market, even if they sell a difference from clinical medicine, even if they sell hope that some atypical practice or some rare knowledge could make a difference. Their knowledge is still invested in products which are inscribed in the order of the supermar-ket in an aisle away from the typical path of the customers whose gaze can be seduced by the average abundance of discounts and special offers. How does E. know that what she takes as truth was not simply desire motivated by suffering, that she has not been seduced by the alternative marketing strategy which managed to turn gluten-free products into a multimillion-dollar market in less than a decade (Levinovitz 2015, 25)? After all, the truth of her self-diagnosis is guaranteed only by the price she has paid for it and by her transformation into a sovereign self able to control her body and life.

Finally, E. finds a doctor from a faraway land who diagnoses her with celiac disease. The doctor tries gently to explain to her that the only treatment is lifelong asceticism, while she is thanking him with startling enthusiasm.

Truth

Parrhesia is able to establish the truth, as far as the parrhesiast is committed to her act.

But the parrhesiastic act is more than just telling the truth, and as far as it is not simply words, the commitment taken on by the parrhesiast cannot be fulfilled by stubborn insistence on words.

Imagine for example that the tyrant responds to the parrhesiast's speech by showing the greatness of his soul (Foucault 2008b, 12). Then the parrhesiast will have to decide whether to continue denouncing his tyranny, to seek reconciliation, to apologize, to recede in silence, or perhaps to show some common sense and recognize that he is not such a bad tyrant after all. The stake of such a decision will not simply be the future behavior of the parrhesiast, the intention or the meaning of her words. The stake will be the real significance of parrhesia, the act itself.

Imagine that the parrhesiast chooses to recede in silence. Then, has she not been silenced by the greatness of the other, whom she accuses of tyranny? Has she not lost the duel with the other, and if she has, was her parrhesiastic act successful? But then imagine that she continues to reproach him, as if he responded with an act of tyranny. Is she not insincere? Does she not insist on words to which she cannot truly commit? If her parrhesiastic act ends in insincerity, was it genuine in the first place? Yet such decisions will not end with the end of the duel. What if, after successfully exposing the tyrant, she is approached by a flatterer who is applauding her? Should she acknowledge his applause, as if she has sought victory rather than truth, or should she reject the applause as well as her victory in trying to preserve the purity of her act?

The commitment of the parrhesiast to her act is a trajectory of such decisions, and none of them can be founded on verifiable knowledge, if only because each decision implies a future that does not depend on the future – the unconditional future of 'I will be the one who will have said the truth.' Indeed, how can one verify phrases like 'I will always love you,' or 'I will never do that,' which nevertheless articulate the unconditional meaning of events that shape entire lives?

But if the parrhesiastic act is successful, because it transforms the speaking self into a subject committed to its truth and because it constitutes the subject of its truth, and if the commitment to the truth of the act consists of an open series of decisions on its real significance, then the act will remain true speech, as far as the parrhesiast reaffirms its real significance by her decisions. The parrhesiastic act will be true as far as its subject is true to her act.[20]

An act of speech can be true not only if it is true to the facts but also if one is true to it. Acts of that type – parrhesia, but also declarations of love, professions of belief, confessions of desire, recognitions of identity, and proclamations of revolution – produce truth which is grounded on fidelity, the object of which disappears without fidelity, and if it is falsified, turns into infidelity rather than into ignorance. The truth of such acts is irreducible to knowledge.

In his later work, Foucault tried to capture the access to truth beyond knowledge by the concept of spirituality (Foucault 2001b, 15–20).

Spirituality is a regime of truth in the sense that it does not define the truth-value of individual statements but rather the conditions of access of truth. As a regime of truth, it is grounded on the assumption that truth is accessible only to a true subject, and that in order to be capable of truth, one must transform oneself; one must become the subject she truly is by reflection, experience, and committed work on oneself. Foucault described spirituality in contrast with the modern regime of truth, which takes the subject's capability of truth as its starting point and defines its access to truth against the background of external negative conditions like madness, ignorance, and immorality (Foucault 2001b, 18).

Parrhesiastic truth belongs to spirituality because it is guaranteed by its transformative effects on the subject and by its price for the parrhesiast, who pays the costs of the risks, even when she does not suffer the consequences of her act.

But what is the price of being true to a conspiracy theory? And if one is committed enough to pay the price of her theory, is it still conspiratorial? Or, since conspiracy theories fail to establish the truth, unlike successful acts of parrhesia, are they merely stories, the price of which one is unwilling to pay?

Notes

1 A state of exception is neither a dictatorship nor illegality because it belongs to the law, although it is beyond the normal legal situations. On the link between conspiracy theories and governmentality based on states of exception, see Fenster 1999, 134.
2 Hazare was arrested together with hundreds of his supporters just before the start of another fast against corruption for disobeying police regulations, and although the arrest was undoubtedly legal, it delegitimized the government even more effectively than Hazare's April 2011 fast. More details see in (Yardley 2011).
3 In that sense, parrhesia is not a speech act, although it is a speech activity (Foucault 2001b, 13).
4 Foucault's comparative analysis of parrhesia and performatives is sketchy because it serves only the purpose of marking off the proper field of parrhesia. So, in order to explain the conditions of possibility of parrhesia as an act of speech, I have adapted the concept of passionate utterances developed by Stanley Cavell (2006). Cavell's concept is also intended to describe acts of speech which are not reducible to performatives – the perlocutionary acts, which Austin left out of his focus. Another reason for adapting Cavell's concept in this context is that parrhesia is an essentially passionate act.
5 This is intended as a reference to the discussion of the dynamic and agonistic structure of parrhesia in Foucault 2008a, 156.
6 The interview is published in Vajsova 2018. For further discussion of the protests, see Georgieva 2017; Medarov 2014.
7 From a different perspective, conspiracy theories are infelicitous because they violate the grammars of normality and plausibility that regulate public denunciations of injustice (Boltanski 2014, 215–21).

8 On the problem of power relations between knowledges see also Birchall 2006, xi.
9 For an innovative analysis of the power effects of that second-order game of veridiction, see the theory of truth developed in Vatsov 2017.
10 If the price of access to subjugated knowledge is minimized by mass production and mass distribution, and if it is sanitized from risk by framing it as entertainment, it turns into popular knowledge. For a definition of the concept of popular knowledge, see Birchall 2006, 21–2.
11 For an argument that describes conspiracy theories as subjugated knowledge, excluded from the games of true and false, and therefore "not even wrong," see Bratich 2008, 2–3, 11. The influential concept of subjugated knowledge introduced by Michael Barkun can be read from a similar perspective (Barkun 2003, 26–7). The transformation of conspiracy theories from legitimate into counter-knowledge is analyzed in Butter 2014, 9.
12 An argument that this conspiratorial attitude is characteristic of late capitalist governments which are trying to compensate for their eroded legitimacy by extending legality, i.e. by developing legal or administrative norms which define in minute detail the interactions between social, political, or economic actors, has been developed in Italian context by Giorgio Agamben (2000, 126–7).
13 I am summarizing just the interviews with experts and scientists broadcasted by Bulgarian national television on 08.05.2010.
14 The concept of seduction can account for the appeal of conspiracy theories, usually explained by their simplicity, their transgressive and ludic nature, or their promise to integrate one into a community of distrust (Fenster 1999, 8, 159, 172, 181).
15 I have rephrased Baudrillard's argument so as to bring it closer to the conceptual framework of this chapter.
16 Rael's Girls describe that effect as emancipation, but it can be just as well described as making the girls enjoy their exploitation. Of course, the Raelian movement condemns forced prostitution, just as non-consensual sex.
17 The story is based on the chapter "My G-Free Journey" in the influential book on the gluten-free lifestyle by Elizabeth Hasselbeck (2008).
18 For a discussion of the relationship between conspiratorial knowledge claims and the perceived impotence of science, see Dean 1998, 8.
19 The description of the different reading of the supermarket aisles is taken from Korn 2010, 134.
20 I am rearticulating the concept of truth developed by Michel Foucault in his later work so as to bring it closer to the concept of truth proposed by Alain Badiou (2005, 327–43).

Bibliography

Agamben, Giorgio. 2005. *The Time That Remains*. Stanford: Stanford UP
Agamben, Giorgio. 2000. *Means Without End*. Minneapolis: Minnesota UP
Agbiotech. 2003. "GMOs for Rael?" Accessed 06.08.2018, www.cabi.org/agbiotechnet/news/3015
Arendt, Hannah. 1972. *Crises of the Republic*. New York: Harcourt
Austin, John. 1962. *How to Do Things with Words*. Oxford: Clarendon

Badiou, Alain. 2005. *Being and Event*. New York: Continuum
Barkun, M. 2003. *A Culture of Conspiracy: Apocalyptic Visions in Contemporary America*. Berkeley: California UP
Baudrillard, Jean. 1990. *Seduction*. Montreal: New World Perspectives
BBC. 2011. "India Activist Anna Hazare Anti-Graft Fast Stokes Anger." *BBC*, 04.07, Accessed 06.08.2018, www.bbc.co.uk/news/world-south-asia-12994855
Birchall, Clare. 2015. "Aesthetics of the Secret", *New Formations* 83: 25–46
Birchall, Clare. 2006. *Knowledge Goes Pop*. Oxford: Berg
BNT. 2010. "Protests Against GMO in the Country." *BNT*, 17.03.2010, Accessed 06.08.2018, http://news.bnt.bg/bg/a/24784-protesti_v_stranata_sreshtu_gmo [БНТ 2010. "Протести в страната срещу ГМО"]
Boltanski, Luc. 2014. *Mysteries & Conspiracies: Detective Stories, Spy Novels, and the Making of Modern Societies*. Cambridge, MA: Polity
Bratich, Jack. 2008. *Conspiracy Panics: Political Rationality and Popular Culture*. Albany: New York UP
Butter, Michael. 2014. *Plots, Designs, and Schemes: American Conspiracy Theories from the Puritans to the Present*. Berlin: Walter de Gruyter
Cavell, Stanley. 2006. *Philosophy the Day After Tomorrow*. Harvard: Harvard UP
Cellucci. 2002. "Cloning and Stem Cell Bill Progressing Well." *Public Library of US Diplomacy*, Accessed 06.08.2018, https://wikileaks.org/plusd/cables/03OTTAWA947_a.html
Chatterjee, Partha. 2012. "The Movement Against Politics", *Cultural Critique* 81: 117–22
Coulter, Jeff. 1987. *The Social Construction of Mind: Studies in Ethnomethodology and Linguistic Philosophy*. Frankfurt.a.M.: Springer
Das, Mona. 2018. "Common Man's Upsurge Against a Common 'Nuisance'", in *Rethinking Ideology in the Age of Global Discontent*, edited by Barrie Axford, Didem Buhari-Gulmez and Seckin Baris Gulmez, 69–86, New York: Routledge
Davis, William. 2011. *Wheat Belly: Lose the Wheat, Lose the Weight, and Find Your Path Back to Health*. New York: Rodale
Dean, Jodi. 1998. *Aliens in America: Conspiracy Cultures from Outerspace to Cyberspace*. Ithaca: Cornell UP
Deleuze, Gilles. 1988. *Foucault*. Minneapolis: Minnesota UP
Deleuze, Gilles and Félix Guattari. 1987. *A Thousand Plateaus: Capitalism and Schizophrenia*. Minneapolis: Minnesota UP
Derrida, Jacques. 2005. *Rogues: Two Essays on Reason*. Stanford: Stanford UP
DSM-III. 1980. *Diagnostic and Statistical Manual of Mental Disorders. Third Edition*. Washington: APA
Fenster, Marc. 1999. *Conspiracy Theories*. Minneapolis: Minnesota UP
Foucault, Michel. 2017. *Subjectivity and Truth: Lectures at the Collège de France 1980–1981*. New York: Palgrave Macmillan
Foucault, Michel. 2009. *Security, Territory, Population: Lectures at the Collège de France, 1977–1978*. New York: Picador
Foucault, Michel. 2008a. *The Government of Self and Others. Lectures at the Collège de France 1982–1983*. New York: Palgrave Macmillan

Foucault, Michel. 2008b. *The Courage of the Truth (The Government of Self and Others). Lectures at the Collège de France 1983–1984*. New York: Palgrave Macmillan

Foucault, Michel. 2004. *"Society Must Be Defended": Lectures at the Collège de France, 1975–1976*. New York: Picador

Foucault, Michel. 2001a. *The Hermeneutics of the Subject: Lectures at the Collège de France 1981–1982*. New York: Palgrave Macmillan

Foucault, Michel. 2001b. *Fearless Speech*. Los Angeles: Semiotext(e)

Foucault, Michel. 1997. *The Politics of Truth*. Los Angeles: Semiotext(e)

Foucault, Michel. 1989. *Archaeology of Knowledge*. London: Routledge

Foucault, Michel. 1981. "The Order of Discourse", in *Untying the Text*, edited by Robert Young, 48–78, New York: Routledge

Garfinkel, Harold. 2002. *Ethomethodology's Program*. Oxford: Romwan & Littlefield

Georgieva, Valentina. 2017. *Dissenting Multitudes*. Sofia: Sofia UP [Георгиева, Валентина. *Множества на несъгласните*]

Hasselbeck, Elizabeth. 2008. *The G-Free Diet: A Gluten-Free Survival Guide*. New York: Center Street

IndLaw. 2011. "PIL Against Anna Hazare on Corruption Charges." The Legal Blog In, 04.22, Accessed 06.08.2018, www.legalblog.in/2011/04/pil-against-anna-haz are-on-corruption.html

Kantor. 2003. "Cloning Claim Puts Spotlight on Quebec-Based Raelian Group." *Public Library of US Diplomacy*, Accessed 06.08.2018, https://wikileaks.org/plusd/cables/03MONTREAL1_a.html

Knight, Peter. 2000. *Conspiracy Culture: From Kennedy to the X Files*. London: Routledge

Korn, Danna. 2010. *Living Gluten-Free for Dummies*. Hoboken: Wiley

Levinovitz, Alan. 2015. *The Gluten Lie, and Other Myths About What You Eat*. Collingwood: Nero

Lyotard, Jean-François. 1984. *The Postmodern Condition*. Manchester: Manchester UP

Medarov, Georgy. 2014. "The Unfolding of the Bulgarian Political Crisis of 2013." *Lefteast*, Accessed 20.08.2018, www.criticatac.ro/lefteast/unfolding-bulgarian-political-crisis/

Melley, Timothy. 2012. *The Covert Sphere: Secrecy, Fiction, and the National Security State*. Ithaca: Cornell UP

News18. 2011. "Probe How Anna Is Drawing Supporters: Congress." *News18*, 04.17, Accessed 06.08.2018, www.news18.com/news/politics/probe-how-anna-is-drawing-supporters-cong-392980.html

PTI. 2011a. "Ramdev Fast: Chronology of Events." *The Times of India*, 06.05, Accessed 06.08.2018, https://timesofindia.indiatimes.com/india/Ramdev-fast-Chronology-of-events/articleshow/8732729.cms?referral=PM

PTI. 2011b. "Nation-Wide Protests Against Anna's Detention." *The Hindu*, 08.16, Accessed 06.08.2018, www.thehindu.com/news/national/other-states/nationwide-protests-against-annas-detention/article2362286.ece?ref=relatedNew

Rael. 2005a. *Intelligent Design: Message from the Designers*. n.d.: The Raelian Foundation

Rael. 2005b. "The Prophet Speaks About Prostitution." *RaeliaNews*, 01.9, Accessed 06.08.2018, http://raelianews.org/news.php?extend.2

Raelgirls. 2018. "Testimonies." Accessed 06.08.2018, www.raelsgirls.com/page.php?4

Rose, Nikolas. 2007. *The Politics of Life Itself.* Cambridge, MA: Princeton UP

Rose, Nikolas. 1999. *Governing the Soul: The Shaping of the Private Self.* London & New York: Free Association

Salla, Michael. 2011. "Wikileaks UFO Cables." *Exopolitics*, Accessed 06.08.2018, www.bibliotecapleyades.net/sociopolitica/sociopol_wikileaks35.htm

TNN. 2011. "India Wins Again, Anna Hazare Calls Off Fast." *The Times of India*, 09.04.2011, Accessed 06.08.2018, https://timesofindia.indiatimes.com/india/India-wins-again-Anna-Hazare-calls-off-fast/articleshow/7921304.cms?referral=PM

Vajsova, Lea. 2018. "Power in Situation." PhD diss., New Bulgarian University

Vatsov, Dimitar. 2017. "What Do We Do When We Say 'This Is True!'." *CAS Working Papers* 9

Yardley, Jim. 2011. "Leader of Corruption Protest Arrested in India." *The New York Times*, 08.16, Accessed 06.08.2018, www.nytimes.com/2011/08/17/world/asia/17india.html?_r=1&ref=world

Conclusion
Against debunking

Conspiracy theories are increasingly becoming a governmental problem. In effect, they are increasingly targeted by techniques of intervention, usually called debunking.

To debunk a conspiracy theory means to identify it as a conspiracy theory and, more importantly, to identify its subjects as conspiracy theorists.

Ideally, their identification should also work as a sanction because those who do not question their own rationality, or at least do not want their rationality to be questioned by others, should reject the theories and isolate or ridicule the theorists.

But debunking as a technique of intervention depends on questionable assumptions:[1]

1 Conspiracy theories are statements about facts.
2 Since conspiracy theorists ascribe truth-value to what is beyond positive knowledge, they believe in it.[2]
3 As far as conspiracy theorists are subjects of belief in what deviates from positive knowledge, they are deviant subjects.

Such assumptions are questionable for the following reasons:

1 Unlike factual statements, conspiracy theories do not have a stable form. They refer to developments rather than to states of affairs and fluctuate with further developments, so they are closer to flows, feeds, or tweets than to texts.
2 Conspiracy theories are often perceived non-seriously or half-seriously, as entertainment or curiosity. And even when they are taken seriously, this is not because their readers are believers but because conspiracy theories seduce them, quite like subliminal messages of choice and chance seduce media audiences or like hopes seduce the clients of contemporary experts on living.

3   Conspiracy theories can be not only oddities but also attempts to articulate what must be known, and cannot be known; for example, whether another social order is possible or what escapes rational calculation. Therefore, their subjects can be defiant rather than deviant.

More importantly, debunking is counterproductive because it ignores the dramatics of conspiracy theories and in effect repairs their infelicity.[3] Rather than statements about facts, conspiracy theories are passing into acts of speech, i.e. infelicitous parrhesiastic acts motivated by suffering and overdetermined by desire which intend to tell the truth against the powerful but articulate instead only meaningless passion.

Since parrhesia is a form of passionate speech, its felicity depends on successfully addressing the other, demanding a response in kind and now. The conditions of felicity of parrhesia also include articulating rebellious knowledge, constituting oneself as a subject of this knowledge, and proving its truth by staying true to the act of its articulation, despite the price paid for it and despite the risks it incurs.

Conspiracy theories are infelicitous acts of parrhesia because they fail to meet one or more of those conditions of felicity. Conspiracy theories can fail to address the other, or fail to elicit actual response in kind; the knowledge they articulate can be commodified, sanitized from risk, and sold at a very affordable price as entertainment, emancipation, or techniques of self-transformation, and the fidelity to the truth of one's act can become almost unfailing by recasting it as a self-reflexive imperative of staying true to oneself.

Debunking can repair the infelicity of a conspiracy theory because it constitutes society as the addressee of the theory and it responds in kind and now by calling for the social excommunication of the theorists, hence associating the conspiratorial act with risk and a price to be paid. More importantly, debunking frames the theory not as ignorance or foolishness but as a stubborn unwillingness to know the truth explainable only by its subject, by the dysfunction, deviation, or abnormality of the subject. Therefore, debunking treats the conspiracy theory as the truth about those who disseminate or consume it; in effect, it constitutes them as subjects of truth, as truly conspiratorial subjects, and it holds the truth about their conspiratorial acts against them as a weapon, even if they try to lose their fidelity.

Therefore, debunking transforms conspiracy theories into veridiction. Of course, it does not verify the knowledge claims of conspiracy theorists but transforms them into supposedly verifiable knowledge about the conspiracy theorists, and in the same stroke, it intensifies their efficacy as passionate acts of speech, the value of which depends on the response they elicit, on the risk run by their subjects, and on the truth effects exerted on those subjects.

Let me illustrate the counterproductive features of debunking with an example. In 2009, a vigilant conservative blogger noticed strange lines in the hair of Barack Obama, president of the United States. The blogger speculated that they could be scars from brain surgery, yet another indication that the president was hiding something. Two years later, another vigilant conservative blogger stumbled upon the post and speculated that the brain surgery was necessary because the president's brain was damaged and that the secrets about his birth or health were so closely guarded that the public would not know anything, even if the brain surgery was done by aliens who replaced him with a cyborg remotely controlled from a distant planet (Hart 2011). The post was widely shared, in the process of its dissemination the question asked by the blogger was cast off as mere rhetoric, and it turned into a statement. Moreover, the timing of the post coincided with the announcement by a future president that he would hire detectives to dig up the truth about the birth of the current president, the publication of an odd-sounding interview with the president's aunt, and the disclosure of official documents on United States contacts with aliens, eagerly anticipated by ufologists. For a couple of weeks, the post about the presidential haircut was among the top 10 results retrieved by a Google search with the words 'Obama' and 'alien.' In effect, the post became viral, and it overflowed into the entertainment sections of tabloids and news outlets ranging from *Fox Nation* to the Bulgarian newspapers. Trying to gain a competitive advantage over the other entertainers, a *Daily Mail* reporter asked the White House to comment (Daily Mail 2011).

Now, imagine that the spokeswoman debunked the question as a conspiracy theory. Since the reporter articulated an impossible knowledge claim, it would be impossible for the spokeswoman to say 'yes' in response. But then, it would make no difference if she was saying 'no.' Moreover, her 'no' could be easily circumvented by transforming the claim into a comment that nevertheless there was something wrong with the president, if his staff could not get even his hair right, as in fact many conservative bloggers did. Therefore, what would make a difference would be not so much the response but the act of responding, and since the claim would have managed to elicit a response from a spokeswoman, it would seem unusually felicitous, or at least less infelicitous than usual. Now, imagine that, being unable to respond effectively, the spokeswoman tried to silence the reporter. Would that not confirm that the reporter had something to say, that he risked being silenced by asking the question? Would the risk not be an indication of a hidden truth? Would the spokeswoman not be contributing to the reputation of the tabloid as a proponent of free speech, as a sort of entrepreneurial parrhesiast?

Since debunking unintentionally stimulates conspiracy theories, they will persist, and the debunkers will be able to explain their surprising persistence only with the need for more debunking. In effect, debunking will achieve nothing but an endless duel with conspiracy theorists.

If this endless duel crossed the threshold of war, it would constitute conspiracy theories as objects of security or medical interventions,[4] and since they are woven into a web of acts of passion, representations of suffering, articulations of subjugated knowledges, stagings of desire, transformations of the self, and courageous speech against the powerful, in trying to capture their object, the interventions would unavoidably deviate into undue acts of medicalization of distrust or policing of dissent. In effect, debunking would not only transform conspiracy theorists into parrhesiasts, it would transfigure the debunkers into tyrants.

Therefore, instead of debunking conspiracy theories, we should try to understand their rationality. Otherwise, democracy is in danger graver than that from any rogue country or wicked dictator because it is founded on popular sovereignty, and if we fail to understand the rationality of conspiracy theories, given their popularity, we can easily end up treating democracy as sovereignty of paranoid people, as government by a mad sovereign. And then democracy will be already dead.

Notes

1 The summary of the implicit assumption of debunking is based on Roeper 2008; Grant 2015; West 2018.
2 For a critique of the assumption that the conspiratorially minded believe in their theories, see Boltanski 2014, 173.
3 From different perspectives, the interventions against conspiracy theories have been criticized for overlooking the existential dimension of conspiracy theories (Boltanski 2014, 183–4), their functions as defensive mechanisms (Adorno 1994, 165), their social functions (Fenster 1999, 82), the anxiety that drives their proponents (Fenster 1999, 82), the commodification that dissociates them from belief (Birchall 2006, 39–40), and the identity forged by the conspiracy theorists (Bratich 2008, 47), and because of that, interventions could achieve only temporary success (Boltanski 2014, 173; Dean 1998, 8). Other relevant critical discussions question the implicit assumption that one should trust the epistemic authorities (Boltanski 2014, 207–8) or that distrust is vital to democracy (Bensaid 2011, 30; Boltanski 2014, 211).
4 For an argument for the medicalization of conspiracy theories as series of individual cases of hysteria, see Showalter 1997, 12. Counterarguments against medicalization are in Adorno et al. 1967, 748; Fenster 1999, 11; Knight 2000, 11; Boltanski 2014, 173. For critiques of social interventions against conspiracy theories, framed by the concept of moral panics, see Bratich 2008, 8–12; Knight 2000, 18.

Bibliography

Adorno, Theodor. 1994. *The Stars Down to Earth*. London: Routledge
Adorno, Theodor, Else Frenkel-Brunswik, Daniel Levinson and R. Nevitt Sanford. 1967. *The Authoritarian Personality*. New York: Wiley

Bensaid, Daniel. 2011. "Permanent Scandal", in *Democracy in What State?* edited by Girogio Agamben et al., 16–43, New York: Columbia UP

Birchall, Clare. 2006. *Knowledge Goes Pop*. Oxford: Berg

Boltanski, Luc. 2014. *Mysteries & Conspiracies: Detective Stories, Spy Novels, and the Making of Modern Societies*. Cambridge, MA: Polity

Bratich, Jack. 2008. *Conspiracy Panics: Political Rationality and Popular Culture*. Albany: New York UP

Daily Mail. 2011. "Mystery scars on Obama's head prompt another question from conspiracy theorists—has the President had brain surgery?" *Daily Mail*, 06.04, Accessed 12.08.2018, www.dailymail.co.uk/news/article-1373780/Mystery-scars-Obamas-head-begs-question—President-brain-surgery.html

Dean, Jodi. 1998. *Aliens in America: Conspiracy Cultures from Outerspace to Cyberspace*. Ithaca: Cornell UP

Fenster, Marc. 1999. *Conspiracy Theories*. Minneapolis: Minnesota UP

Grant, Richard. 2015. *Debunk It!: How to Stay Sane in a World of Misinformation*. San Francisco: Zest Books

Hart, Ben. 2011. "What's That Huge Long Scar on Obama's Head? And Is That Why We Can't See His Birth Certificate?" *Escape Tyranny*, Accessed 16.01.2012, www.escapetyranny.com/2011/04/03/whats-that-huge-long-scar-on-obamas-head-and-is-that-why-we-cant-see-his-birth-certificate

Knight, Peter. 2000. *Conspiracy Culture: From Kennedy to the X Files*. London & New York: Routledge

Roeper, Richard. 2008. *Debunked!: Conspiracy Theories, Urban Legends, and Evil Plots of the 21st Century*. Chicago: Chicago Review

Showalter, Elaine. 1997. *Hystories: Hysterical Epidemics and Modern Culture*. New York: Picador

West, Mick. 2018. *Escaping the Rabbit Hole: How to Debunk Conspiracy Theories Using Facts, Logic, and Respect*. New York: Skyhorse

Index

98   *Index*